The Gold Fields of the Klondike

FORTUNE SEEKERS' GUIDE TO THE YUKON REGION OF ALASKA AND BRITISH AMERICA

THE STORY AS TOLD BY LADUE, BERRY, PHISCATOR AND OTHER GOLD FINDERS

BY
JOHN W. LEONARD

With Maps, Diagrams and Illustrations

ORIGINALLY PUBLISHED BY:
LONDON:
T. FISHER UNWIN
CHICAGO:
A.N. MARQUIS & COMPANY

REPUBLISHED IN 1994 BY:
WHITEHORSE, YUKON:
CLAIREDGE
211 Wood Street, Whitehorse, Yukon Y1A 2E4 Canada

ISBN 0-9698723-0-5

This drawing, from sketch made on the spot by New York Journal artist at the Grand Hotel, San Francisco, shows bags, belonging to Clarence J. Berry, which contained over $84,000[1] in nuggets and gold dust. As they stood on the table, they measured 8-1/2 x 13-1/2 inches.

(1) In 1994, this much gold would be worth very close to $2,100,000.

INTRODUCTION

The Gold Fields of the Klondike is as precious as the metal that lured thousands of people to the Yukon Territory in search of their fortune back in the 1980s.

Perhaps one of the first "guide books" to the Yukon Territory ever written, *The Gold Fields of the Klondike* was published in 1897, just months after news of the great gold strike in the Klondike reached the world.

Little is known about the author, John W. Leonard. He provides only this brief glimpse of himself:

> "My own acquaintance with mining covers a third of a century, beginning with a toilsome and perilous trip to the Echuca diggings in Australia in 1864, but after all those years, during which I have been in many mining districts all over the world, I am free to confess that the Klondike discoveries outclass all of the great gold strikes I ever knew or heard of."

By no means a brilliant writer, Leonard did manage to put together a comprehensive package of information that no doubt served many a would-be gold seeker well.

Leonard provides details about everything from what to wear to what kind of weather to expect to how to get the gold out of the ground. He also included maps, photographs and illustrations to help the reader along.

Although there is no way to know how many copies of this book rolled off the presses back in 1897, we do know that not many copies survived.

However, thanks to people like former Yukon Territorial Councillor and Dawson City businessman, George Shaw, who provided his copy for this reprint, a whole new generation will have an opportunity to glimpse, and, perhaps, to feel the essence of one of the world's great gold rushes — the Yukon Gold Rush of 1896-1898.

For the sake of authenticity, we have left the text exactly as it appeared in print — errors, poor grammar, misspellings and all. The illustrations are also faithful copies of the originals, although we have changed their placement to locate them more closely to the text they enhance.

The original book contained a few photographs, but we have selected a larger number from the Yukon Archives to more broadly illustrate the story that lay behind John Leonard's words. Many were actually taken in 1897.

The blending of the original book with photographs from the gold rush days, the writing of cutlines and the addition of a note here and there are the work of Mary Shiell, a freelance writer and editor with an abiding interest in the north. Her careful selection of appropriate photographs that were unavailable to John Leonard has added greatly to the potential enjoyment of today's reader. What may have seemed a little mundane when viewed some 100 years after the fact is given meaning and relevance by her additions. She has wisely left Leonard's original text unaltered, relying on the readers to gain the impact of those years through the eyes of a raconteur who was there and who was able to write about it well.

CONTENTS

ILLUSTRATIONS

KLONDIKE GOLD
A miner and his tools of trade — a pick, a shovel and a sluice box.
(Yukon Archives/Vancouver Public Library Collection)

FORWARD

By Dick North*

One of the amazing aspects of *The Gold Fields of the Klondike*, authored by John W. Leonard, is the speed with which it was put together. The book is a tract of "how to" and informational items presented with a specific market in mind — those persons bent on going to northwest Canada in the gold rush of 1897 and 1898. And, since word of the huge gold strike really did not filter south until the summer of 1897, it was little short of a miracle that Leonard was able to get the book under a copyright of that year.

Equally amazing is the fact that the contents of this work were generally accurate, considering it must have been a rush job. A book like this is worthwhile for the reason of its timeliness. It is an enlightening experience to read something that has been written "when it happened", as against pursuing material that descends upon us via reams of secondary sources.

The value of surveying an event from the perspective of those persons on hand is to ask why so many men and women uprooted themselves in the mad dash to get to the diggings in the first place. Most students of history would think that the stampeders wanted to get to the fields to accumulate gold, yet close scrutiny of this book points to the contrary. I quote Leonard: "Some of the successful miners did not even own claims. They have been working for other men for $15 a day and thus have accumulated small

---

* Dick North is an internationally respected author whose interests have kept him researching and writing about the north. He is perhaps best known for his book "Mad Trapper of Rat River," which has been reprinted seven times and made into a movie. He is also recognized as an expert on Jack London, the famed U.S. author who spent time in the Yukon during the gold rush and based several of his works on events he encountered while in the Klondike.

fortunes. The smallest sack (of those belonging to miners off the first ship from the Klondike) is $3,000 held by C.A. Brannan, of Seattle, a happy fellow only 18 years old." He worked for wages.

One wonders immediately what three thousand dollars represented in purchasing power in 1897. The answer is provided in facts presented in the book. For example, a Harvard graduate seeking employment in Seattle in 1894 found that $7 a week was the most he could earn. In other words, in a year he would have made $350 — as compared to Brannan earning ten times that much in half a year. Thus, a man who wanted to make a stake in a hurry could go to the Klondike and come out relatively wealthy working for wages — if he stayed away from the high-cost temptations offered in downtown Dawson City.

To pursue the point a little further, the value of gold mined in those years in the Yukon Territory ran to roughly $16 an ounce. The 1897 gold price of $16 divides into the 1994 gold price of about $380 U.S. at about 25 times. Fifteen dollars for a day's work (in 1897) would be about $375 for a day's work in 1994. For a 10-hour day, that translates into a present wage of about $37.50 per hour, fairly close to today's earnings.

Not to belabor the subject, if we scan prices of the 1890s in the Klondike region, it presents a more comprehensive overview of the economic picture. The book offers these facts and figures.

The currency used in the Yukon River valley was an odd combination of pelts, gold dust and dollars. Each item of exchange often represented the affectations of the occupation of the holder. A trapper sold the former, miners used gold, and dollars were a medium used by all. One of the more interesting tie-ins is mentioned in the book. If a customer entered a trading post and asked the price of an object, the trader might quote in skins. The basic unit of value was the marten or fox pelt, which had a value of about $1.25. In other words, if one wondered about the price of fifty pounds of flour, it could be priced at five skins, or $6.25 in normal parlance. Five pounds of sugar cost one skin, and five yards of drill were one skin. Making the conversion to today's values, one skin or five pounds of sugar would be valued at about $32.25.

Prices were high in Dawson City, obviously because of the freight. The lowest monetary unit was "four bits", the price of even the most insignificant item. A newcomer once complained about this flat bottom price to the proprietor of a store. The storekeeper just shrugged his shoulder and said, "It's not the item; it's the freight in getting it here."

Anecdotes crop up in *Gold Fields* that tend to puncture one's illusions about the gold camp. Ethel Bush, who married the highly successful miner Clarence J. Berry before accompanying him to the Klondike, stated that when she went into Dawson City, "... it was in such a rowdy state that it was impossible for me to to go to my meals, and I had to have them sent to me." She added that people, "... who follow on the heels of the good, steady-going, hard-working miners are among the worst." However, Mrs. Berry liked working on the creeks with her husband, and although she enjoyed it in the winter, summer was another thing. "It is damp," she said, "the water is bad, it gets very hot, and the mosquitoes are awful."

Mrs. Eli Gage viewed the Klondike region in another light than did Mrs. Berry. She is quoted as saying, "It is wonderful how fascinating the life on the frontier becomes. The man or woman who gets a taste of it and succeeds and thrives by it rarely gets into anything else." The fact that her husband was the auditor for the North American Transportation and Trading Company certainly could not have hurt her optimistic outlook.

The Gold Fields of the Klondike encompasses all sorts of historical data that are intriguing. One such item refers to the fact that the miners on Bonanza Creek decided to remeasure all of the claims. Somehow, the men selected for the job managed to substitute a rope that measured forty feet for one that measured fifty feet. This created fractions of claims, which were promptly staked. Chaos reined until the Canadian government brought in an engineer, William Olgilvie, to straighten out the mess. He resurveyed the creek and adjusted the claims to the satisfaction of most all concerned. He later became Commissioner of the Yukon Territory.

The information and advice offered in the book is remarkable for its candor. Unlike many similar publications, this one does not flinch when it describes the working conditions in the Klondike. One miner is quoted as saying, "An ounce of physical culture is worth ten pounds of classical and scientific training." This is summed up in the text: "The requisites, then, are a sound body, perseverance, temperance and a cool head, and a man is well equipped for the journey."

The book is not without its errors, such as the consistent mistake of referring to George M. Carmack as George McCormack. Also, distances and locations are often distorted. But, for gold rush afficionados it is well worth the read.

(Dick North is the curator of the Jack London
Interpretive Centre in Dawson City)

PREFACE

Some books are written for the same purpose that rural newspapers are established—"to fill a long-felt want." The volume now presented, however, aims rather to fill a new-felt want, which, just now, is pressing and wide-spread, for complete and reliable information about the new land of gold, for the word "Klondike" now fills every mouth and every ear.

The subject being timely, the writer has endeavored to apply the advantages of an experience covering years of life in mining camps in different parts of the world, in such a manner as to answer the questions daily being asked about the latest El Dorado and gold mining methods.

The story of the Klondike discoveries here told is that of those who saw them and were part of them, and the facts in regard to Alaska, Northwestern Territory and the Yukon Region have been gathered from the last and latest resources of information.

For those going to the mines the preparations to be made, the outfit required, the details of the route, and the methods of prospecting and mining are minutely described, and the mining laws, both of Canada and the United States, are given, so that the prospector may know his duties as well as his rights.

For those who stay at home the story will be none the less interesting, as the Klondike and its doings will long continue to be an important subject of discussion.

— *John Leonard*

AN EARLY GOLD SHIPMENT

This mound of sacks of gold awaits shipment to the "outside."
Many hours of pleasant speculation could pass thinking about
what one could do with all this wealth — the "spell of the Yukon"
as Robert Service called it.

(Yukon Archives/Vancouver Public Library Collection)

Chapter I

Gold On The Klondike

Wealth-Laden gravel in a new El Dorado.

Gold for the digging! No piece of news that wires can flash will set more hopes to work than this; for gold means money, ease, comfort, freedom from thousands of cares. What if the road to it be long, full of peril, adventure and perhaps suffering, if a year or two of strenuous labour will bring to one who has toiled, unrequited, for years, the means of future independence? Given a sound constitution, a stout heart, and American grit, mere physical obstacles will have little weight so that gold in plenty rewards the pursuit, and the hard knocks of experience are paid for in want-dispelling affluence.

Shorter road to wealth

All industry is prosecuted for the purpose of securing a living, and is mere drudgery unless there be a hope that a surplus over a mere living can be secured to guard old age from poverty. Therefore nearly every active man is seeking some shortened road by which wealth can be secured. None of these is so attractive as that which leads to virgin gold — gold which can be had by the mere act of delving for it and washing from it the earth or dirt by which it has been hid but not contaminated.

Gold attracted thousands

Gold in California attracted hundreds of thousands of people to make the tempestuous voyage around Cape Horn, or the shorter but not less perilous trip over the miasmatic Panama route, to the Golden Gate, and thence to the foothills of the Sierra, where they delved and tunnelled and panned and flumed, many to find only disappointment, but a large number also to find that which they sought — a golden fortune.

Gold in Australia made thousands venture into the heart of an unknown country, much of it desert, and at Ballarat, Sandhurst, Bendigo or over the mountains to the Echuca diggings, and now thousands are seeking it in West Australia.

Gold in South Africa has opened up a very large area of the Dark Continent to civilized settlement and is adding millions annually to the world's wealth.

Gold has been found during recent years in many parts of the United States, but mostly in quartz mines which take machinery and large capital to develop them properly. Many a man has sighed for days like those of '49, when a man could take a pick, a shovel, a pan and a stout heart and seek his fortune with a reasonable expectation of finding it. Thousands have longed to repeat the experience of the Argonauts of that famous period, and dig for gold dust and nuggets in the earth.

The chance has come again! And the goal of opportunity is the Klondike, in British America, near the Alaskan boundary. From there we hear wonderful reports, which, extravagant as they may appear, are confirmed from many sources, official and otherwise, to such an extent as to make the wonderful richness of the region beyond dispute. Only a comparatively small portion of the auriferous area has been prospected in any systematic manner, but every indication points to the fact that there, in the frozen North, is a country whose riches exceed "the wealth of Ormus and of Ind," and of which are told, by staid officials and matter-of-fact pioneers, stories which sound like the romances of Scheherazade.

Except to the pioneers who found the way to the new diggings in the fall of 1896 and winter of 1897, the name, even, of the Klondike was unknown to all except to a very few white persons. It was omitted from a majority of the maps and spelled "Chandik" in nearly all the others, and if the name had been spoken in any company it would have aroused no interest.

Klondike suddenly famous

All this was changed in the middle of July, 1897. On the 15th the steamer "Excelsior" arrived at San Francisco, bringing about forty passengers, from St. Michaels, Alaska, among whom were fifteen who had won fortune in the Klondike district. The story of these men appeared in the principal papers of the country, but many of the journals made little of the story — evidently doubting its

THE TREASURE STEAMSHIP EXCELSIOR AND J.F. HIGGINS, HER CAPTAIN

truth, because the statements made appeared so extravagant.

Two days later the steamer "Portland" arrived at Seattle, Wash., with sixty-eight passengers from the Klondike. Of these not one had brought less than $5,000 and one or two had over $100,000. Their stories were even more wonderful than those narrated by the passengers of the "Excelsior." They told of thawing out frozen gravel in the cold arctic winter, of washings yielding as high as $150 to $200 to the pan of "dirt," of poverty changed to riches, of hardships requited by opulence, of great suffering from poor fare and a rigorous climate, but large returns to all who worked.

Stories verified

These stories have been more than verified by subsequent reports, some of which are from government officials, the Dominion chief of internal boundary survey, the governor of the Canadian Northwest Territory, as well as many others, of the United States and Canada. It is unquestionably true, beyond dispute, that in the Canadian Northwest Territory and Alaska, and in fact for hundreds of miles, in the valleys of the Yukon and its tributaries, is an auriferous region as large as or larger than that of California, part of which, at least, is richer than any district ever known in the history of placer mining.

It is not to be wondered at, therefore, that the people of this country have been filled with excitement, and that there is a general demand for information about the Klondike discoveries; the character of the Klondike country and adjacent regions of Northwest Territory and Alaska; the climate, resources, food supplies and other information as to things to be done, seen and endured;

the route to be taken, requisite outfit and supplies, cost of living, chances of success, etc. It is known that the climate is a rigorous one, and there is a general desire to know the impediments and dangers of winter in that region, and the obstacles to be met with on the way.

Many inquirers also desire to know something about gold mining in general, the processes and methods pursued and the details of the miner's life. To answer these questions in a plain, concise manner, so as to meet the needs of the inquiring public, is the object of the chapters which follow.

Chapter II

The Klondike Discoveries

How adventurous pioneers found fortune in the river banks

Ever since the United States acquired Russian America by purchase, and named it "Alaska" after a suggestion of Charles Sumner, there have been rumors of great mineral wealth there. In southeastern Alaska there is the famous Treadwell Mine, on Douglas Island, opposite Juneau, a wide vein of low grade ore, in the reduction of which a 240-stamp quartz mill, the largest in the world is used.

Several years ago there were rumors of important alluvial gold deposits on the Upper Yukon. The headwaters of the river were discovered by the Hudson Bay Company, in 1840. A government exploration of the region on behalf of the United States was made by Dr. W.H. Dall and Frederick Whymper, who wintered on the Upper Yukon in 1865. The first prospecting party went over the Chilkoot Pass in 1880, and since then miners have gone by that route in increasing numbers. In 1886 there were numerous parties attracted to the Yukon diggings, but the results were not very encouraging. William C. Greenfield, who completed the account of the Yukon River District for the United States census of 1890, reported: "Mining cannot be called a success on the Yukon, up to the present time. Since the first excitement in 1886, there have been but few instances of individuals taking more than $2,000 for two or three seasons' work."

Years ago the Hudson Bay Company established, about eight miles northwest of the mouth of the Klondike, a trading post which was called Fort Reliance, since abandoned. Its exact location is latitude 64° 13', longitude 138° 50', or fifty statute miles east of the boundary line of 141°. About forty miles northwest, down the river, is the mouth of Forty-Mile Creek, where Fort Cudahy is located, and about 240 miles further down the Yukon is Circle City. At the latter place, and on Forty-Mile Creek, the principal activity in placer mining on the Yukon has centred.

George McCormack[1]

One of those who had been engaged in mining at the Forty-Mile camp was George McCormack, a native of Illinois. He went to the Upper Yukon region in 1887 as a member of the surveying party of William Ogilvie, chief of the Canadian Internal Boundary Survey. He left that employ and became a prospector and miner, took an Indian squaw wife of the Takuth tribe, known locally as the "Sticks", and from that fact became known among the white Yukon miners as "Stick George." The "Sticks" have a village at the junction of the Klondike and Yukon, and McCormack, who had not done well in Forty-Mile, heard from the Indians rumors of large gold deposits on the branches of the Klondike. He went up to the first branch, and early in August, 1896, located a placer claim. Then, to get provisions, he worked cutting logs for a mill at Forty-Mile camp, and at the end of August returned to his claim with his Indian wife and brother-in-law and set to work. The gravel had to be carried in a box on his back from thirty to one hundred feet and everything had to be done in the crudest and most laborious manner, yet the three, working very irregularly, washed out $1,200 in

(1) Throughout the book, Leonard refers to George Carmack, one of the discoverers of gold in the Klondike, as George McCormack. Carmacks, Yukon is named after this historic Yukoner.

DISCOVERY . . .

This is George Carmack's placer gold claim affidavit on the Bonanza Creek (Rabbit Creek) claim that sparked the Klondike gold rush on August 17, 1996. Note how one could mistake the signature for the name "McCormack".

(Yukon Archives / A.C. Johnson Collection)

GEORGE CARMACK

(Yukon Archives/A.C. Johnson Collection)

KATE CARMACK

(Yukon Archives / A.C. Johnson Collection)

eight days. McCormack says, with reason, that if he had possessed the proper facilities he could have washed the same amount of gravel in two days.

McCormack let his friends at Forty-Mile know of his luck. Clarence J. Berry and others went early. Many other miners did not go with the rush, thinking the report only another of the disappointing hoaxes so often set on foot in mining communities. Most of those who went to the new camp were novices — "tenderfeet" as they are called, or "Chee Chacoes" (new men) in the Yukon dialect — whose hope was greater than their experience. These pioneers of the Klondike named the tributary on which McCormack had located his claim "Bonanza Creek", and it has fully borne out its designation. Then another branch, which flows into Bonanza Creek before it reaches the Klondike, was explored by F.W. Cobb, a Harvard graduate, and he and his partner, Frank Phiscator, a farmer from Baroda, Mich., located their claims on this creek. They found their claims washed $10 to the pan of surface dirt.

"Frank", said the Harvard man to his partner, "this creek is studded with gold from here to head-waters. We will call it El Dorado." And thus was appropriately named the famous brook which has made many fortunes in the past few months and is making others today.

The first dozen or so of prospectors who arrived on the ground were followed in a few days by 150 more, who came in on the steamer "Ellis," and a stampede from Circle City, Forty-Mile and other camps was the result of the find. Still it was the "tenderfeet" who showed the greatest faith in the future of the developments. William D. Johns, writing from Dawson City under date of June 18, gives a most graphic statement of the subsequent history of these wonderful gold discoveries up to that time. He says:

"Few had much faith in the new region even after they

SKOOKUM JIM AND TAGISH CHARLIE
Striking it rich . . . Skookum Jim (in suit second from right) with his wife and child. Tagish Charlie stands at the end of the deck in a white shirt.

(Yukon Archives / D. Bohn Collection)

were on the ground, and in spite of the rich prospects on
the surface it was generally regarded as a 'grub-stake'
strike on which one might succeed in getting a winter
outfit. A little later, however, the prospects found on the
river called forth the half-skeptical remark that 'if it goes
down it is the greatest thing on earth.' Then a few began
to believe in the new diggings, but many old miners even
yet would not stake out claims, thinking the creek too
wide for gold. A number of side gulches along the
Bonanza were staked, among them El Dorado, which was
rich in gravel near the mouth. But so little faith was
manifested in the region that claim holders could not get
'grub' from the stores in exchange for their prospects.
There was a general fear that these might be only 'skim
diggings.'

Fabulously rich pay dirt

"In December bed rock was reached on No.14 El
Dorado and fabulously rich pay dirt was found. Then
more holes went down in a hurry. Everywhere were
discovered prospects on bed rock ranging from $5 to $150
to the pan. The gold was nearly all coarse. Still the
greatness of the strike was not realized. Some of the best
claims were sold by their owners for a few hundred or a
few thousand. Drifting was carried on by the usual winter
process of 'burning,' and the pay dirt taken out as rapidly
as possible under the difficulties of intense cold. Pans as
rich as $500 were discovered, and nuggets containing
gold worth as high as $235 were brought to light. Claims
jumped up enormously in price, but still many men sold
for a small part of the value of their holdings. They
seemed wholly unable to realize their good fortune.
Doubts were still expressed about the dumps holding out
to the prospects.

"Then the test — sluicing — came in the spring when the ice melted and the water ran down from the hills. Then the wildest hopes of the toiling miners were realized. Despite the lateness of commencing work and the scarcity of men about $1,500,000 was taken out of El Dorado alone. On some of the richer claims men who secured ground to work on shares — 50 per cent — cleared $5,000 to $10,000 apiece in from thirty days' to two months' drifting. As high as $150,000 was drifted out of one claim, the other sums becoming less. From seventy-

A GOOD PAN
Six miners grouped around a gold pan counting nuggets. A $45.00 pan was deemed a "good pan".
(Yukon Archives / Vancouver Public Library Collection)

five feet of ground on Nos. 25 and 26, El Dorado, $112,000 was taken, or $1,500 per running foot, and the pay not cross-cut, for it frequently runs from vein to vein, being in places 150 feet wide.

$500,000 for a claim

"Ground has sold here this spring for over $1,000 a running foot, or at the rate of $500,000 for a claim of 500 feet. Men on whose judgment reliance can be placed and who base their opinion on what their own ground and that of others has yielded, tell me that there are claims here from which over $1,000,000 will come. Last winter men on 'lays' (percentage)[1] left 50-cent dirt because they had better insight and only a limited time before spring to get out ore. Owing to the large number of men on 'lays' the production of almost every claim is known, and no overstatement is possible, since so many are interested in the amount of gold produced. As soon as sluicing was fairly under way the price of claims jumped again and but few would sell. It might almost be said that no one would part with a claim on El Dorado. On Bonanza, where the pay, except on a few claims, is not as rich as on El Dorado, owners who had looked in vain for the $5, $10 and $150 pans, which were plentiful on the rival creek, were disgusted with their moderate gains and were willing to sell. Thus many claims having 20- to 50-cent dirt and three to seven feet of it were sold. On the boat which takes this letter down the Yukon will be many men, some of them having been in this country only a few months when the strike was made, who will take with them to the mint from $10,000 to $500,000, the result either of

(1) A "lay" is a practice whereby a miner may work a claim owned by someone else by pledging a certain percentage of the gold recovered to the owner. Ten percent is common today, but is a negotiated figure that depends on the richness of the claim.

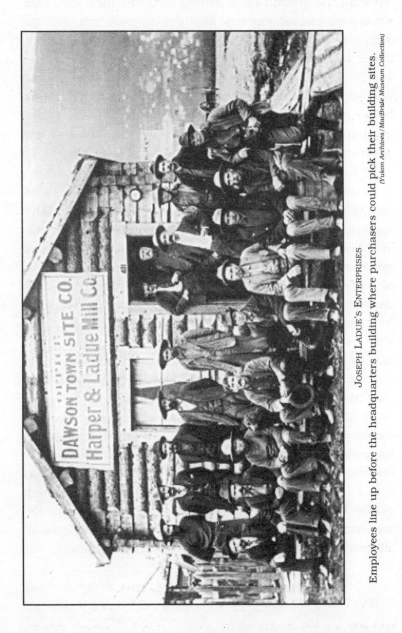

JOSEPH LADUE'S ENTERPRISES

Employees line up before the headquarters building where purchasers could pick their building sites.

(Yukon Archives / MacBride Museum Collection)

working the ground or of selling out. The men who sold were paid almost entirely out of their own ground, the men who bought taking the dumps and these, when sluiced, paying for the claims and leaving a handsome margin for the purchasers. In some instances enough gold was rocked out to make a first payment on the claims before sluicing was possible. Many of these men, to my personal knowledge, had neither money nor credit to get 'grub' with last fall."

Ladue lays out town of Dawson

In September Joseph Ladue laid out Dawson City, applying for a town site patent on his claim. It is on the Yukon River, below the mouth of the Klondike, and fifteen miles below the Bonanza Creek mines. It had a population of 3,500 in June, but has a much larger one now, as people from Juneau, Sitka, Forty-Mile and Circle City have gone into Dawson in large numbers, besides those who are on their way or have already reached there from different parts of the the United States and Canada.

Before the winter set in quite a large population had located in the Klondike district. The population increased faster than the supplies, and until the arrival of boats in the early spring short rations were the rule, and prices for supplies were exceedingly high. Claims were prospected and partly worked, the method being to build fires on the spot to be excavated and, when the ground was thawed out for a foot or so, to dig it out and pile the "pay dirt" on the dumps ready to be panned or sluiced in the spring, after various modes which will be described elsewhere.

Wonderful stories of wealth

There have been many wonderful stories told of sudden wealth acquired in gold mines in various fields, and some miners have made fortunes as great as those recently achieved by the pioneers of the Klondike, but there never was a district where all the claims located turned out to be paying ones, as was the case with those located on El Dorado and Bonanza Creeks in the fall of 1896.

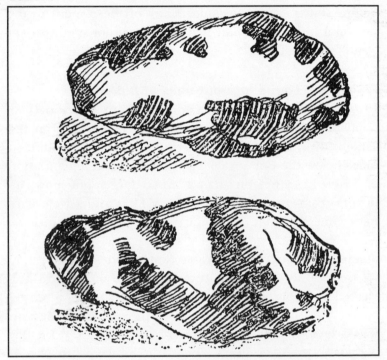

This is a nugget imbedded in a pebble. It is valued at $157[1], and came from El Dorado Creek. The white indicates gold, and the two pictures show the upper and under sides, actual size.

All who were in the district during the winter of 1896-97 made money. Those who had claims sank shafts which revealed "pay dirt" at a few feet below the surface and became richer as the lower ground was reached. This fact became so apparent that many of the miners flung aside dirt

(1) More than $4,000 U.S. dollars by 1994 gold values.

A pan of dirt, in miner's parlance, contains two shovelfuls of the usual "California pattern" miner's shovel. Fifteen cents to the pan is considered "good wages." The small bottle shown on the left-hand side shows, actual size, the gold found in one pan, amounting to $153.70 in value. The bottle on the right-hand side, which is also actual size, shows the gold from one pan of dirt, and amounting to $300[1]. Both pans of dirt came from Claim No. 5 above Discovery, Bonanza Creek, owned by Clarence J. Berry.

(1) In 1994 U.S. dollars, about $7,500.

yielding from 50 cents to $5 a pan in order to get to the fine black sand stratum on bed rock which yielded an average of $50 per pan for a depth of from one foot to eighteen inches.

Great riches uncovered

That the uninitiated may have some idea of the riches thus uncovered it may be well to state that a "pan" of dirt is two miners' shovelfuls, and that in ordinary placer mining a claim is considered quite good when it yields from ten to fifteen cents to the pan: "bit dirt" as they say in California, where the word "bit" is an equivalent term for the "York shilling" or 12 1/2 cents.

In the Klondike region the ground for a considerable distance above bed rock is always frozen, even in summer, and in the winter the surface earth is also frozen. This makes the work of the miner very laborious, and makes it necessary that ground should be rich in order that it be made to pay.

Those who had no claims located, or who, having claims, were without provisions, found it easy to get work for others at from fifteen to twenty dollars per day. Even at those figures there were not many who could be prevailed upon to work long for wages. As soon as they had a "grub stake" ahead most of these hired men struck out for themselves. Some, however, worked the winter through and found themselves possessed of a substantial sum as the reward of their industry. When spring arrived and the snow began to melt there was plenty of water for "sluicing" the dirt which had been dug out during the winter, and it was then that owners of claims found themselves rich as the result of a few days' clean-up.

All brought back gold

Quite a number of the more fortunate, leaving their partners in charge, went down the Yukon as soon as navigation opened, and from St. Michaels Island in the Bering Sea, sailed for San Francisco on the steamer "Excelsior," belonging to the Alaska Commercial Company, or for Seattle on the steamer "Portland," belonging to the North American Transportation and Trading Company. It was from these Argonauts of 1897 that the people of the United States and Canada first heard of the wonderful gold discoveries on the Klondike. All of them brought back substantial evidences of success in gold dust and nuggets. The "Excelsior" arrived in San Francisco on Wednesday, July 15. The names of the returned miners with the amounts of gold they brought and the value of the claims they left behind them in the Klondike district area as follows:

	Brought from Alaska[1]	Value of Claims[1]
T.S. Lippy and wife	$65,000	$1,000,000
F.G.H. Bowker	90,000	500,000
Joseph Ladue	50,000	500,000
I.B. Hollinshed	25,000	
William Kuiju	17,000	
James McMann	15,000	
Albert Galbraith	15,000	
Neil Macarthur	15,000	
Douglas Macarthur	15,000	
Bernard Anderson	14,000	35,000
Robert Krook	14,000	20,000
Fred Lendesser	13,000	
Alexander Orr	11,500	
John Marks	11,500	
Thomas Cook	10,000	25,000
M.S. Norcross	10,000	
J. Ernmerger	10,000	
Con. Stamatin	8,250	
Albert Fox	5,100	35,000
Greg Stewart	5,000	20,000
J.O. Hestwood	5,000	250,000
Thomas Flack	5,000	50,000
Louis B. Rhoads	5,000	35,000
Fred Price	5,000	20,000
Alaska Commercial Company	250,000	

Total, $439,000

(1) When adjusted to today's gold values by a factor of more than 25, these sums become princely.

Mrs. Gage returns

Two days later, on Friday, July 17, the steamer "Portland" arrived at Seattle, with passengers and a ton and a half of gold. One of its passengers was Mrs. Eli Gage, a daughter-in-law of Lyman J. Gage, a secretary of the treasury, whose husband is Auditor of the North American Transportation and Trading Company, and is located at Fort Cudahy, N.W.T., forty three miles below Dawson City on the Yukon River. The other passengers, who came from the Klondike, were: Clarence J. Berry and wife, Miss E. Nelson, Frank Phiscator, F. Miller, A. McKenzie, C. Anderson and wife, C.A. Branan, O. Finsted, H. Anderson, W. Sloane, J. Johnson, C.E. Neyer, A. Gray, G. Worden, R.H. Blake, William Stanley, W. Sims, R. McNulty, J. Halterman, J. Anderson, J. Desroche, T.J. Kelly, V. Lord, F. Pellinger, J.E. Poucher, N. Mercer, F. Moran, J. Clements, H. Olsen, A. Proteau, H. Dore, M. Kelly, H. Granthier, M. Hall, B.F. Purcell, C. Silverlock, H.Coteland, J. Bergwin, F. Fabhr, J. Moffett, C.H. Loveland, Inspector Strickland and wife, Sergeant Hayne, Sergeant Engel, Corporal Newbrook, Constable Jenkins, Constable Telford, C. Encher, C. Anderson, J. E. Fairburn, Miss P. Block, Miss E. Sedick and five steerage.

Today they are wealthy

"These men," said Captain Kidston, of the "Portland," "are every one what the Yukoners call 'Chee Chacoes' or newcomers, and up to last winter they had nothing. To-day you see them wealthy and happy. Why, on the fifteen days' trip from St. Michaels I never spent a pleasanter time in my life. These fortunate people felt so happy that anything would suffice for them, and I could not help contrasting them with the crowd of gold hunters I took with me on the last trip up. They were grumblers, without a cent in the world, and nothing on the boat was good enough for them. Some of these successful miners do not even own claims.

The treasure ship "Portland"

They have been working for other men for $15 a day, and thus have accumulated small fortunes. Their average on this boat is not less than $10,000 to the man, and the very smallest sack is $3,000. It is held by C.A. Branan, of Seattle, a happy young fellow just 18 years old. There is no country on earth like the Yukon."

Considerable excitement about the Klondike has resulted from the stories told by the lucky passengers of the "Excelsior," but when the much larger number that came by the "Portland" were heard from, bringing over $1,000,000 in gold dust and nuggets to add force to their statements, the gold fever broke out all over the country, and a rush has begun which will land in the Yukon valley all who can be carried there this summer, while thousands more will go in the spring of 1898.

Chapter III

Pioneers of the Klondike

Stories of those who were in the first rush to the Bonanza district

The facts in regard to the Klondike adventurers read like romances, but they agree so well and are so thoroughly fortified by the large receipts of treasure that their truthfulness is not open to suspicion even.

Clarence J. Berry and wife

Perhaps the most romantic story is that of Clarence J. Berry and his wife "the bride of the Klondike." Mr. Berry was a fruit raiser in Fresno Country, California. He found it a hard task to make a living there. In 1894 he heard of gold finds in the Yukon region, in far-off Alaska. He had just $40 of his own and managed to borrow $60 more on the promise of heavy interest. He went to Juneau, where he found a number of others who had arrived there with the view of crossing over the mountains. A party of forty was organized, among whom was Berry. It was early spring, when they started out each with a load of supplies and furs. Indians packed these to the top of the Chilkoot Pass. The winter journey in the mountains proved too much for many in the party and many gave up in despair and turned back. When the lakes were reached and boats built the water voyage was begun. The melted snow had swollen the streams, and in Lake Bennett the whole outfit of supplies went down. This discouraged all but three. Berry, with magnificent strength and a hero's courage, was one of the three who with a meager supply of food pushed on, and after nearly a month's toilsome journey reached Forty-Mile Creek, penniless. He went to work for

CLARENCE J. BERRY
With his partner he took out over $130,000 last season, and his
claim is not one-tenth worked. He also owns other rich claims.

MRS. CLARENCE J. BERRY
The "bride of the Klondike" in winter costume.

Fortymile in 1896. Spring break-up of the Forty-Mile River and the Yukon River is visible.

(Yukon Archives / D'arcy Edward Collection)

others and later for himself, with indifferent success, but
acquired a faith in future fortune on the Yukon which
made him determined to find it or die in the attempt. In
the fall of 1895 he concluded to return to Selma, Fresno
Country, where he had left a young woman who had
promised to be his wife. When he returned he found Miss
Ethel D. Bush prepared not only to redeem her promise
but also to go with him and share his fortunes in the
frozen North, although he pictured to her the hardships
as well as the hopes that belonged to life in that region. In
March, 1896, they were married, and in April the couple
reached Juneau on their unique wedding trip. They had
little capital, but two brave hearts. They went by boat to
Dyea, the head of navigation, and from there over the
mountains by dog team. At night they slept under a tent
on a bed of boughs. Mrs. Berry's garments resembled her
husband's. They were made of seal fur with the fur inside,
and came over her feet like old-fashioned sandals. Over
them were pulled a pair of gum boots. Over her shoulders
was a fur robe and her hood was of bearskin. This all
made a great weight of clothing, but she trudged by her
husband's side, and in June, three months after they
were married, they reached the camp at Forty-Mile Creek.
There Berry worked until in September, 1896, he was told
of McCormack's find up the Klondike. There was much
excitement at "Forty-Mile" over the news, though the
experienced miners for the most part ridiculed the idea
that anything good would be found "over there on the
Klondike." Berry, however, was one of those who believed
that something good had been found, and his wife helped
him to get ready for his trip into the new district, Mrs.
Berry remaining at Forty-Mile. Two days later, Berry was
in the Bonanza district, where it had been decided that
500 feet on the river Bonanza Creek should constitute a

claim. His location was "Claim No.40 above the Discovery" — which means that thirty nine 500-foot claims intervened between his ground and the original one staked out by George McCormack.

On El Dorado Creek

Soon Mrs. Berry went to Dawson City, which had just been started. Mr. Berry built a house, and was joined by his wife. He secured Claim No.5 above the Discovery on El Dorado Creek and there found rich dirt varying from $2 to the pan just below the surface to $50 to the pan on the bed rock. Mr. Berry hired men at $15 a day and from the $130,000 which he took out before he left he paid out $22,000 to his miners. He still owns his claims on the Bonanza and El Dorado, besides interest in many others, and has a fortune which will reach into the millions. Mrs. Berry will remain in Fresno, but Mr. Berry will return to manage his mines, which he left in good hands to be worked during his absence. Mr. Berry's El Dorado claim was one of the richest that had been worked on the creek during the winter and spring. The principal part of his $130,000 came from thirty "box-lengths" of dirt. A "box-length" is fifteen feet long and twelve feet wide. In one length he found a pocket of $10,000. In another length was a nugget weighing thirteen ounces — next to the largest found in the diggings.

Refuse work at $1.25 per hour

All winter men received $1.25 an hour on the Berry claim, but at these wages not a pick would have been raised had it not been for the fact that nothing can be done during the severe cold but pile the gravel on the dump ready for washing in the spring, and many of these men did not have enough food to keep them at this work on their own claims. Every day was pay day. Mr. Berry settled with his men every night merely by taking a pan of dirt, washing it out with water obtained from melted ice, and weighting out each man's time in gold nuggets. His expenses averaged from $100 to $150 a day all winter, but this was a small sum for a place whence every man expects to return home a millionaire, and where a man with less than $50 in his dust sack is looked upon as broke.

Although Mr. Berry is proud of his plucky wife he did not give her a cent of "pin money" out of his riches while they were on the Klondike. He did not need to do so; for the intervals of housekeeping she would go to the dump and wash out a few pans of dirt for herself. In this way she secured over $10,000 as her personal perquisites for sixteen months of a bridal "outing" in the frozen Northwest.

Champion pan for one month on El Dorado Creek $300
brought home by Clarence J. Berry

JOSEPH LADUE

Joseph Ladue

One of the best known of the Klondikers is Joseph Ladue, the founder of Dawson, N.W.T., the metropolis of the Yukon, at the mouth of the Klondike

He is forty-three years old, and lived, until 1882, at Schuyler Falls, Clinton County, New York, and was a farm hand, working for H.H. Lobdell, until he left and went to the Black Hills in search of gold. He met with considerable success at first, but afterwards lost every dollar in a speculation in Deadwood. From there he went to the northwest, finally reaching Alaska. He was at Sixty-Mile for several years, running a saw mill and store there. It was a good investment, although Mr. Ladue found great difficulty in running it, because men preferred mining, even when he was paying his hands $15 per day. But his returns were proportionate to his expenses, as the cheapest lumber he ever sold brought $100 per thousand feet, and planed lumber double that sum. After the Klondike boom broke out the price of rough lumber went up to $150 per thousand, and the demand far exceeded the supply.

No sooner had the richness of Bonanza and El Dorado creeks been indicated than Mr. Ladue laid out the town site of Dawson, entering the land under the Canadian laws, and having it surveyed into lots. The most eligibly located of these lots are now selling at $5,000 each and upward. Mr. Ladue has also become possessed of valuable mining interests, and has already accumulated a substantial fortune. He came back on the "Excelsior" and went on a visit to Schuyler Falls, N.Y., as a guest of H.H. Lobdell, his old employer.

When Mr. Ladue lived at Schuyler Falls he became engaged to Miss Anna Mason, the daughter of prosperous parents. The latter objected to his marriage because of his lack of means, and he went west; but the young woman remained faithful to him and correspondence was kept up. When Mr. Ladue returned to Schuyler Falls the preparations for the wedding were at once inaugurated, and on July 29 the two were united in marriage, and another romance was added to the story of the Klondike.

Frank Phiscator and F.W. Cobb

Two of the most fortunate of the Klondike miners are Frank Phiscator and F.W. Cobb. They are partners in the mines and were the first to locate on El Dorado Creek.

Frank Phiscator was a farmer's boy in Michigan, and was born at Baroda, in that state, thirty-five years ago.

JOSEPH LADUE'S SAWMILL

His father died, and Frank, tiring of the farm, went west, and got employment in Yellowstone Park, carrying horseback mail over a sixty-mile route. Later he went to live in the state of Washington and there, by hard work and thrift, accumulated about $3,000. Then he went back to Michigan, but did not find the people there as cordial in manner as those he had left in the west, so he again turned his face toward the setting sun, and when he had reached Seattle he heard reports about mines on the Yukon which attracted him. He went there and struck up an acquaintance with F.W. Cobb, the two agreeing to share with each other. Then when McCormack located on the Bonanza, the two were there with first rush to the new field.

F.W. Cobb was born in New England and was graduated from Harvard University. In 1894 he went to Seattle, but times were fearfully hard, and he worked about, in various capacities, making no more than $7 a week. Finally he sent back east to his relatives for money and with it struck out for the Yukon, meeting up with Frank Phiscator at Forty-Mile and going with him to the Bonanza District. When they reached there Phiscator

FRANK PHISCATOR, OF BARODA, MICH.
He went to the Klondike and made a fortune in a year.

prospected on the Klondike above Bonanza, while Cobb went up the latter stream until he struck the branch to which he afterwards gave the name "El Dorado."

Struck it rich

A little experimental panning of dirt convinced him that he had "struck it rich" and he located a claim of 1,000 feet, being entitled by right of discovery to twice the usual allotment of ground. Then he hurried down the Bonanza end at its mouth and found Phiscator returning, disconsolate, from a fruitless search for the yellow metal up the main stream. To him he communicated the news of his find, and the two returned to the El Dorado, where Phiscator located alongside his partner's discovery claim.

The two have made fortunes. In the spring "clean-up" of their claims the first forty days brought Phiscator's share of the gold to $96,000, which he brought with him on the "Portland" to Seattle. He left Mr. Cobb in charge of the claims, but will return in the spring and let Cobb come "outside." They have millions in sight on their claims.

The noteworthy thing about these two is that neither of them had any mining experience before they went to Alaska in 1896, and they made their fortunes in less than a year.

The Stanleys and Wordens

Among the most wonderful stores of a sudden rise from poverty to affluence is that concerning the Stanleys and Wordens, who formed a company of four working in partnership in the Klondike gold fields, consisting of William M. Stanley, his son Samuel, and the brothers Gage and Charles Worden. None of them had any previous mining experience.

William M. Stanley is a gray-haired man, well along in years. He lived in a humble home in the southern part of Seattle with his wife and several children. He conducted a little book store in an out of the way corner of that city, but found it hard to make a living, for times were hard in Seattle as well as all other parts of the country from 1893 to 1896. In March of the latter year Mr. Stanley got together all the money he could, borrowed a little more from his son William, who was working elsewhere, and with his 23 year old son Samuel, started for the Yukon country on the steamer "Alki', from Seattle for Dyea

WILLIAM M. STANLEY   GAGE WORDEN

On the "Alki" the Stanleys met two young men, Charles and Gage Worden. They came from Sackett's Harbour, N.Y., to seek their fortunes in the west, but found nothing better to do than to work on a milk ranch at small pay. They too, were on their way to the Yukon.

The four men knew nothing about mining, and had even less real conception of the hardships of travel and living in the frozen mountains of the North.

Went over Chilkoot Pass

Laboriously they toiled over the Chilkoot Pass route with their burdens, and after several weeks of wearisome and dangerous travel they reached the mouth of the Stewart River. The four had agreed to work together and divide the proceeds of their joint venture. Up the Stewart they went and finally found a drift near the mouth of the McQueston Creek, an affluent of the Stewart. They built rockers and worked on the dirt in that vicinity, getting out from $10 to $20 per day. Soon the "pay" became less, and the party, after seeking for better locations for a time without success, started for Forty-Mile, and rested en route at Sixty-Mile (so called because the mouth of the river so named is about sixty miles above Fort Reliance). There they met a miner whom they had previously befriended, and who told them of the rumors of McCormack's great "find" on the Klondike. They reached the mouth of that stream and looked about for a favorable location. Next day the steamer "Ellis" arrived from Forty-Mile with one hundred and fifty excited miners aboard. The Stanleys and Wordens joined in the rush for the new diggings and on El Dorado Creek made locations on claims Nos. 25, 26, 53 and 54 above the Discovery Claim of F.W. Cobb. They began work on Claims 25 and 26 and were soon satisfied that they had a good thing. They then went to work to prepare for a long winter of experience and hardships, and found all they wanted before spring. They built a log cabin and made it as snug as possible, and then all four put in their time sinking prospect holes in the gulch. The rest of the intensely interesting story is best told in the graphic description given by William Stanley after his arrival at Seattle on the "Portland".

"I tell the simple truth when I say that within three months we took from the two claims the sum of $112,000. A remarkable thing about our findings is that in taking this enormous sum, we did not drift up and down stream, nor did we cross-cut the pay streaks.

"Of course, we may be wrong, but this is the way we are figuring, and we are so certain that what we say is true that we would not sell out for a million. In our judgment, based on close figuring, there are in the two claims we worked, and Claims 53 and 54, $1,000 to the lineal foot. I say that in four claims we have at the very least $2,000,000, which can be taken out without any great work.

Pay dirt in every creek

"I want to say that I believe there is gold in every creek in Alaska. Certainly on the Klondike the claims are not spotted. One seems to be as good as another. It's gold, gold, gold, all over. It's yards wide and yards deep. I say so because I have been there and have the gold to show for it. All you have to do is to run a hole down, and there you find plenty of gold dust. I would say that our pans on the El Dorado claims will average $3, some go as high as $150, and believe me when I say that, in five pans, I have taken out as high as $750 and sometimes more. I did not pick the pans, but simply put them against by breast and scooped the dirt off the bed rock.

"Of course, the majority of those on the Klondike have done much figuring as to the amount of gold the Klondike will yield. Many times we fellows figured on the prospects of the El Dorado. I would not hesitate much about guaranteeing $21,000,000 and should not be surprised a bit if $25,000,000 or even $30,000,000 was taken out.

"Some people will tell you that the Klondike is a marvel, and there will never be a discovery in Alaska which will compare with it. I don't believe it. I think that there will be a number of new creeks discovered that will make wonderful yields. Why, Bear Gulch is just like El Dorado. Bear Gulch has a double bed rock. Many do not know it, but it's a fact, and miners who are acquainted with it will tell you the same thing.

Gold black as a cat

"The bed rocks are three feet apart. In the lower bed the gold is as black as a black cat, and in the upper bed the gold is as bright as any you ever saw. We own No. 10 claim, below Discovery, on Bear Gulch, and also Nos. 20 and 21 on Last Chance Gulch, above Discovery. We prospected for three miles on Last Chance Gulch, and could not tell the best place to locate the Discovery claim. The man making a discovery of the creek is entitled by law to take a claim and take an adjoining one, or in other words, two claims; so you see he wants to get in a good location on the creek or gulch. Hunker Gulch is highly looked to. I think it will prove another great district, and some good strikes have also been made on Dominion Creek. Indian Creek is also becoming famous.

"What are we doing with all the money we take out?"

"Well, we paid $45,000 spot cash for a half-interest in Claim 32, El Dorado. We also loaned $5,000 each to four parties on El Dorado Creek, taking mortgages on their claims, so you see we are well secured.

"No, I do not want any better security for my money than El Dorado claims, thank you. I only wish I had a mortgage on the whole creek.

No more poverty

"We had a great deal of trouble in securing labour in prospecting our properties. Old miners would not work for any price. We could occasionally rope in a greenhorn and get him to work for a few days at $15 a day. Six or eight miners worked on shares for us about six weeks, and we settled. It developed that they had earned in that length of time $5,300 each. That was pretty good pay, wasn't it? We paid one old miner $12 for three hours work and offered to continue him at that rate, but he would not have it, and he went out to hunt a claim of his own. My son Samuel, and Charles Worden are in charge of our interests in Alaska. Gage Worden and I came out, and we will go back in March and relieve them. Then they will come out for a spell. Gage goes from here to his home in New York State to make his mother comfortable.

"I am American by birth, but of Irish parents. I formerly lived in western Kansas, but my claim there was not quite as good as the one I staked out on the El Dorado Creek."

Mr. Stanley's family had a hard time getting along during the fifteen months the father and brother were away, but they will never know poverty from this time on.

Mr. and Mrs. Lippy

Mr. and Mrs. T.S. Lippy, formerly of San Francisco, also came down on the "Excelsior." Mrs. Lippy went North with her husband in April, 1896, their destination being Forty-Mile, where Lippy and his brothers had a fine paying claim. She was one of the first white women to make the journey over the big divide and says she did not find the trip very difficult. Mrs. Lippy denied emphatically the stories of starvation in the mining districts of the far North.

"We enjoyed life exceedingly at Forty-Mile", she said. "To be sure, our amusements are limited, but there are a number of women there now, and we try to make it as pleasant for each other as possible. Everybody is doing well. The story of suffering among miners is news to me. I never saw nor heard of any suffering. We were skimped for some articles, but there was always plenty to eat. Everybody had a good supply of something, and if one ran out of bacon it was the customary thing to exchange with some neighbour who was short of flour or beans. That is the way we all did and we got along very comfortably."

Mr. Lippy brought with him $60,000 in gold dust, and left claims in the Bonanza district worth $1,000,000. His brothers, whom he left in charge, have been equally fortunate. This book could be filled with the stories of the returning miners. So far as the character of the diggings in the Klondike they all agree. These are certainly the most wonderful gold discoveries ever known.

Marvellous riches

Not only those who have returned, but also many who remain, testify to the marvellous riches of the country. The following characteristic letters were written from Dawson City to Juneau friends.

Burt Shuler, writing from Klondike under date of June 5, says:

"We have been here but a short time and we all have money. Provisions are much higher than they were two years ago and clothing is clean out of sight. One of the A.C. Co.'s boats was lost in the spring, and there will be a shortage of provisions again this fall. There is nothing that a man could eat or wear that he cannot get a good price for. First class rubber boots are worth from an ounce to $25 a pair. The price of flour has been raised from $4 to $6 and it was selling at $50 when we arrived, as it was being freighted from Forty-Mile. Big money can be made by bringing a small outfit over the trail this fall. Wages have been $15 per day all winter, though a reduction to $10 was attempted, but the miners quit work . . . Here is a creek that is eighteen miles long, and as far as it is known, without a miss. There are not enough men in the country today to work the claims. Several other creeks show equal promise, but very little work has been done on the latter. I have seen gold dust until it seems almost as cheap as sawdust. If you are coming, come prepared to stay two years at least; bring plenty of clothing and good rubber boots."

Here is a letter from another enthusiast:

"Klondike, May 27, 1897

"Friend Bill:-

"We landed here the 17th and went on a stampede the next day, and have just got back. I came through the camp and saw a good many friends. I saw Burt; he has a claim on Bonanza Creek. Billy Leake has bought a claim on El Dorado; the claim is supposed to be worth a million. There are thirty-four claims on the same creek which seem to be as good. Bonanza is good, but not so rich. There are 100 claims on Bonanza which are good, and there are other creeks which give good pay. Bill, it is the best camp I ever saw. Wages are $15 a day; everything is high; gum boots are selling at $25. I look for a new strike this summer, as many men are out prospecting, and it is the best gold country I ever saw. I wish you were here; we will make a stake if we stay with it; I will have something before winter. If you come in this fall don't start after the 15th of August; one can make more here in one year than he can in ten out there. There will be work the year round; wages may be cut to $10, but I don't think it; I can go to work at any time and as long as I wish for $15. It will pay to bring anything here which can be carried in; the demand is good and prices such that there is money in anything that can be brought in. Money will hardly buy claims here now, but men can often get in on a 'lay'. I know men who took 'lays' since Feb. 1 and made enough to go out with as high as $20,000 apiece.

"Andy Hensley."

Fears gold will have to be demonetised

Oscar Ashby fears that gold will have to be demonetised, for he says in a letter dated May 18 from Circle City:

"Hereafter address all letters to Klondike, N.W. Territory. I would have stayed in Alaska. but when I heard of McKinley's election I pulled my freight, for I know that meant gold. I tell you one thing, if they find a few more El Dorado and Bonanza creeks, they will have to demonetise gold. Some of the kings are hurrying out to spend their money before that is done. However, I am going to take chances on mine."

Circle City deserted

Another letter says:

"Circle City is deserted, every one having gone to Klondike, where the richest strike of the kind ever known in any country was made last fall. The stories told are not exaggerated. One hundred dollars to the pan is very common. One can hardly believe it, but it is true, nevertheless.

"El Dorado is staked off into claims for eight or ten miles, and every claim so far has shown up big. One claim was sold for $100,000 three days ago. Bonanza is good also, and two or three other gulches close by show up well. Every camp in the Yukon valley is deserted for Klondike. Wages there are $15, while $12 is the prevailing rate here. No one wants to work for wages, but all are prospecting. This is undoubtedly the best poor man's country in the world today. A very hard country to live in on account of the mosquitoes and poor grub, but healthy and a show to make a ten-strike. We heard that McCollough, formerly of the Juneau Hotel, had been drowned while shooting the White Horse Rapids; don't know whether there is any truth in it, as he was behind us. A number of parties were swamped and lost their outfits, but escaped with their lives. The trip is anything but one of pleasure, as you will find if you ever make it."

"Fred Brewster Fay."

JOSEPH LADUE, FOUNDER OF DAWSON CITY
(Yukon Archives / Joseph Ladue Collection)

Chapter IV

Joseph Ladue's Story

The Klondike strike described by the owner of Dawson

The true story of the Klondike has never been fully told, not because the history of this eventful strike was not preserved, but because there were few men present at its birth. I mean by that, few men who went into the region with the real discoverers.

For fifteen years I traded throughout that entire section, and coupled with my town to town commerce a saw mill industry, and I have no doubt that many others were equally familiar with the territory. But it remained for a man from Nova Scotia, a Robert Henderson, to turn over the dirt that led to the opening up of what I and others consider the most marvellous mineral discovery in the world. I will begin with Henderson's discovery and carry the reader right through the excitement up to the very population of Dawson, a town which now has 4,000 souls, military protection and forty families of men, women and children.

Finds gold in gold bottom

It was on the 24th of August[1] when Henderson, who had been prospecting for four years in Indian Creek, a tributary of the Yukon, found himself in another little stream bed known as Gold Bottom, near the Yukon, the high water having driven him out of Indian Creek. He was prospecting around, hoping to find something as good as the ground seemed to contain. After a time he panned out

---

(1) George Carmack made his discovery on August 17th. and registered it in September. The author is likely referring to happenings that occurred in July, prior to the discovery, rather than in August.

ROBERT HENDERSON
Henderson travelled from Nova Scotia to the Klondike.
(Yukon Archives / Hare Collection)

a little gold and put in a sluice box or two. In a very short time he ran out of supplies and went back to Fort Ogilvie, where I was stationed, and reported the find to me. I lost no time getting myself in readiness to proceed to the spot at once, and by the 28th of August I had two men and four horses in Gold Bottom. In the meantime Henderson drifted down to the mouth of the Klondike in a small boat, and found George McCormack, an old friend of his, who was fishing for salmon. Hunting up his friends when there was anything in sight seemed to be one of Henderson's best traits. He got McCormack up to Gold Bottom, where he located a claim, prospected around a while, and started back across country for the mouth of the Klondike River, a distance of twenty miles.

That trip was destined to play an important part in the events which followed, for through it occurred one of the big finds. McCormack took with him two Chilkat Indians, and the three men went off in the direction of Bonanza Creek, where the three men went off in the direction of Bonanza Creek, where the white man struck gravel that went $2.50 to the pan. According to our mining laws in Canadian possessions, the discoverer can locate an extra claim for himself as a reward for making the find. So McCormack took up two locations and the Indians one each. They set to work at once and took out $120 in gold in three days with little else than a pan. Then they came down to Fort Ogilvie and reported the find.

The rush for the mines

That report which was spread by McCormack, had the immediate effect of sending a thrill of excitement along the Yukon, from the head-waters down to Forty-Mile and Circle City. As though by magic, the trails were sprinkled with pack mules, and the river was dotted with small craft coming up or going down to the new diggings, as the case may be. In less than ten days there were about 150 miners at work on new claims.

Strangely enough, and as if by some great good fortune, I had come down the river about the same time McCormack left Gold Bottom, and had picked out a town site where Dawson City now stands, a little more than a mile from the Bonanza Creek claims. In this respect I was very fortunate, as it now stands right in the midst of what is called Bonanza Gold Mining District, and all claims are so recorded. As a matter of fact there is no other suitable place for a town site, and I consider myself lucky in getting hold of it. I hold 178 acres, while the remaining

GEORGE DAWSON
The man after whom Dawson City is named.
(Yukon Archives / Joseph Ladue Collection)

twenty-two are the property of the Government. The Yukon at that point is 600 yards across and about thirty five fathoms deep, with natural advantages for protection of craft. Dawson City is just below the mouth of the

Klondike River. I named it after George Dawson, the man who established the boundary line that is now recognized as the correct line dividing Alaska from the Northwest Territory. It runs due north from Mount St. Elias to Point Demarcation to the 141st meridian. That, of course, cuts all the present locations, with the exception of those at Forty-Mile, out of United States possessions. There is no cause for dispute on that score at all. It is purely a Canadian section, and is under the Canadian laws.

Trickery of greed

Just as soon as the rush began at Bonanza Creek the miners called a meeting, and in order that the claims be relocated and made sure of, it was decided to measure them all off with a rope and reset the stakes that defined them. Somehow or other the men selected to make the measurements slid in a forty instead of a fifty foot rope, and thus made the claims from fifty to one hundred feet short in the total. In other words, they were condensed, and the intervening ground was literally grabbed. This state of affairs incensed the miners so that when they made the discovery of how the measurements were conducted, they petitioned William Ogilvie, the Dominion Land Surveyor, to come up to Bonanza Creek at once and settle the complications that were arising. He resurveyed the whole group of claims and the matter was then adjusted to the satisfaction of all hands. But even now some of them are a little short. The custom in taking up placer claims is to locate 500 feet the way the valley lies, and then run across from base to the base of the foothills. In the Bonanza Creek it is 800 feet to the base lines.

The Dominion Land Surveyor is also a magistrate, and has the power to take sworn testimony, which he did in the case of the false measurements. The men who had engaged in the work, both of playing short rope and

The finding of a nugget would almost drive the prospectors crazy. The largest was picked up by Bert Hudson on Claim 6, and was worth $257. The next best was secured by J.J. Clements in Indian Creek, and went for $235. There are two hundred claims in El Dorado Creek, and not one of them has failed to produce large returns. In the Bonanza there are thirty-nine claims, and they too, are wonderfully rich, and constantly improving. There is four and a half miles of pay gravel in one streak, and from all indications more to come.

$94,000 from a forty foot patch

A miner by the name of Alex MacDonald took out $94,000 from a forty foot patch of ground only two feet thick. He employed four men to do the work and consumed but twenty-eight days. That gravel went $250 to the pan, and was in Claim No. 30, El Dorado Creek.

Different men have cleaned up from $175,000 to $50,000 in fine gold, and all of it was done during three months of the past winter. Out of El Dorado alone came $4,000,000, and at least $1,000,000 from Bonanza Creek. How much more there is in it is impossible to say, but to all appearances the whole district is full of gold waiting to be taken out.

When the ice began to melt this summer another rush began. Forty-Mile City and Circle City were depopulated last winter, and the new rush came from the South, Seattle, Juneau and all the states. Steamer after steamer has left the Pacific coast bound for the mines, but for the life of me I do not know where they are to get supplies. All the boats now obtainable by the Alaska Commercial Company are worked to their fullest capacity, and it takes thirty five days in good weather to get to Dawson from San Francisco.

Now that I have touched the subject of transportation I may as well go deeper into it. There seems to be a general

JOSEPH LADUE'S HOME

belief that anybody can go up to El Dorado and pick up a hatfull of gold anytime. Perhaps there was a chance to do that at first, but since then the mines have filled up with practical, scientific mining men, and nothing is lying around loose. The nearest point to get supplies at anything like civilization rates is Juneau, but beyond that city is a stretch of territory that an inexperienced man had best avoid, and particularly at this season of the year.

I have been careful not to exaggerate in the least bit, and I hope some day to see the region of the Klondike a thriving mining and commercial centre, but I trust no one will be foolhardy enough to attempt the trip now. If you must go, follow my advice and do not start until the 15th of March, and then go by way of Seattle to Juneau or Dyea, walk overland thirty miles to the headwaters of the Yukon and sail from there 400 miles down stream to the city of Dawson, which by this time next year will have 20,000 people and be able to care for them.

Joseph Ladue

Chapter V

High authority confirms the richness of the Klondike strike

The news from official sources in regard to the Klondike discoveries is fully as sensational in character as that given by the returning miners.

No man living has a closer acquaintance with that region than William Ogilvie, Dominion Surveyor and Chief of Internal Boundary Survey, who, with a field force, has been in the Northwest Territory for over ten years, definitely locating the line of 141° west longitude, which forms the boundary line dividing Alaska from the British Northwest Territory. He is a man highly respected in the far northern country, where, in addition to his official duties, he is often called upon to settle mining questions as an arbitrator whose fairness is beyond dispute. Mr. Ogilvie, since the Klondike discoveries, has made an official report in which he says:

"The name Klondike is a mispronunciation of the Indian word or words 'Thron-dak' or 'duick', which means plenty of fish, from the fact that it is a famous salmon stream. It is marked 'Ton-dak', on our maps."

After telling of the discovery of gold there in 1896 by G. McCormack, Mr. Ogilvie presages considerable trouble and confusion in the near future from the lack of system in making out claims. He says: "When it was fairly established that Bonanza Creek was rich in gold — which took a few days, for Klondike had been prospected several times with no encouraging results — there was a great rush from all over the country adjacent to Forty-Mile. The town was almost deserted; men who had been in a chronic state of drunkenness for weeks were pitched into boats as ballast and taken up to stake themselves a claim, and claims were staked by men for their friends who were not in the country at the time. All this gave rise to much confliction and confusion, there being no one to take charge of matters. The agent not being able to go up and attend to the thing, and myself not knowing what to do, the miners held a meeting and appointed one of themselves to measure off and stake the claims and record the owners' names, for which he got a fee of $2.00, it being of course understood that each claimholder would have to record his claim with the Dominion agent and pay his fee of $15. I am afraid that a state of affairs will develop in the Klondike district that will worry some one. Naturally, many squabbles will arise out of those transactions when the claims come to be considered valuable and worked, and those, together with the disputes over the size of the claims, will take some time to clear off. Many of the claims are said to be only 300 and 400 feet long, and of course the holders will insist on getting the full 500, and it is now probably impossible that they can without upsetting all the claimholders on several creeks. Many of them will be reasonable enough to see things in their proper light and submit quietly, but many will insist upon what they call their rights."

Riches of the Klondike fields

In reference to the richness of the Klondike fields, Mr. Ogilvie says that the rich fields in that district, such as Miller, Glacier and Chicken creeks, have been practically abandoned for the Klondike. Men cannot be got to work for love or money, and the standard of wages is $1.50 an hour. Some of the claims are so rich that every night a few pans of dirt is sufficient to pay all the hired help.

Mr. Ogilvie complains sorely of the need of some kind of court to settle the various claim disputes that are continually arising between the miners. He says that the force and virtue of the miners' meetings prevailed until the mounted police made their appearance, after which sneaks had full swing.

The morality of the Klondike would seem to be of a much higher order than is usually found in new mining camps, the presence of the mounted police seeming to have a most salutary effect. Mr. Ogilvie seems to regret it, for he says:

"The man who was stabbed here in November has quite recovered, but may never have the same use of his back as of old, having received a bad cut there. His assailant is out on bail, awaiting the entrance of a judge to try him. As the police are here, there will be no lynching; it is almost a pity there will not."

The liquor traffic

Mr. Ogilvie takes up the subject of the liquor traffic also, saying: "The impression of the best men here, saloon men and all, is that the liquor trade should be regulated, that no one but responsible parties should be allowed to bring liquor in; men in business here of established reputation and having an interest in the country and the retail traffic, licensed as in the Eastern provinces, giving licenses to men of fair character only. Now any loafer who can gather enough money to secure a few gallons and a few glasses and wants to have an idle time, sets up a saloon. In my opinion it is imperative that the business be brought under control at once, or it may develop phases that will be at least annoying in the future."

Mr. Ogilvie announces the location of a quartz lode showing free gold in paying quantities along one of the

C. MILNE, PANNING FOR GOLD ON NO. 2 BONANZA
(Yukon Archives/McLennan Collection)

creeks. The quartz has tested over $100 a ton. The lode appears to run from three to eight feet in thickness, and is about 19 miles from the Yukon River. Good quartz has been found also at the head of a branch of the Alsek River near the head of the Chilkat Inlet, inside the summit of the coast range in Canadian territory; also along Davis

Creek in American territory. The hills around Bonanza Creek also contain pay quartz. Copper in abundance is found on the southerly branch of the White River, and silver ore has been picked up in the creek flowing into Bennett Lake. Mr. Ogilvie says that the placer prospects continue to be more and more encouraging and extraordinary.

"It is beyond a doubt," he says, "that three pans of different claims on El Dorado turned out $204, $212 and $216, but it must be borne in mind that there were only three such pans, though there are many running from $10 to $50."

Governor McIntosh

The executive of Northwest Territory, in which the whole of the Canadian Yukon country is located, is Governor H.C. McIntosh. Speaking of the discoveries in the Klondike region, he said in a newspaper interview:

"We are only on the threshold of the greatest discovery ever made. Gold has been piling up in all these innumerable streams for hundreds of years. Much of the territory the foot of man has never trod. It would hardly be possible for one to exaggerate the richness, not only of the Klondike, but of other districts in the Canadian Yukon. At the same time the folly of thousands rushing in there without proper means of subsistence and utter ignorance of geographical conditions of the country should be kept ever in mind.

Golden waterways

"There are fully 9,000 miles of these golden waterways in the region of the Yukon. Rivers, creeks and streams of every size and description are all rich in gold. I derived this knowledge from many old Hudson Bay explorers, who assured me that they considered the gold next to inexhaustible.

"In 1894 I made a report to Sir John Thompson, then premier of Canada, who died the same year, at Windsor Castle, strongly urging that a body of Canadian police be established on the river to maintain order. This was done in 1895, and the British outpost of Fort Cudahy was founded.

"I have known gold to exist there since 1889, consequently upon a report made to me by William Ogilvie, the government explorer. Many streams that will no doubt prove to be as rich as the Klondike have not been explored or prospected. Among these I might mention Dominion Creek, Hootalinqua River, Stewart River, Liard River and a score of other streams comparatively unknown.

"It is my judgment and opinion that the 1897 yield of the Canadian Yukon will exceed $10,000,000 in gold. Of course, as in case of the Cariboo and Cassiar districts years ago, it will be impossible accurately to estimate the full amount taken out.

"There is now far in excess of $1,000,000 remaining already mined on the Klondike. It is in valises, tin cans and lying loose in saloons, but just as sacredly guarded there and apparently as safe as if it were in a vault. Already this spring we have official knowledge of over $2,000,000 in gold having been taken from the Klondike camps. It was shipped out on the steamships Excelsior and Portland.

"Incidentally I may say we have data of an official nature which leads us to believe that the gold output of the Rossland and Kootenai districts for 1897 will be in excess of $7,000,000. I should have said, and I have no hesitancy in asserting, that within the course of five years the gold yield of the three districts named will exceed that of either Colorado, California or South Africa."

Chapter VI

The Yukon Region

General description of the
great gold fields district

The great central district of Alaska and the western portion of the British Northwest Territory are drained by one of the largest streams on the American Continent. It is over 2,200 miles long, of which distance about 1,500 miles is in Alaska and the remainder in British America, the dividing line between the two being the 141st degree of longitude west from the Greenwich meridian.

The portion of the region which is in United States territory formed the Sixth Census District in the U.S. Census for 1890. Up to that time the whole region was principally known to fur traders, although a few miners had gone in previously for about six years. The settlements, according to the census, were 58. Of the total population of 3,912 there were 2,099 males and 1,813 female; 2,082 natives and 1,830 foreign. Racially distinguished, there were 202 whites, of whom 193 were male, and 9 female; 127 mixed breed, of whom 59 were male and 68 female; and 3,583 Indian, of whom there were males 1,847 and females 1,736.

These figures of seven years ago do not give much indication in regard to present conditions of population. Since then many prospectors and miners have gone into the country, and the whites now outnumber the Indians in that region.

Yukon known by other names

The great Yukon River is not known by that name for its entire length. The Pelly and Lewis Rivers, both large streams, unite, and at their confluence in British territory, about longitude 137° 30' west, form the Yukon.

The Lewis River is the better known of these two streams, from the fact that since 1884, it has been used as a highway from southeastern Alaska to the Yukon gold fields. Its length, from Lake Lindermann, one of its chief sources, to the junction with the Pelly, is about 375 miles, and it lies entirely within British territory with the exception of a few miles of the lakes at its head.

The Pelly River takes its rise about Dease Lake, near the headwaters of the Stikine River, with a length of about 500 miles before joining the Lewis to form the Yukon River. The union of these steams forms a river varying from three fourths of a mile to a mile in width. For many miles there is on the northern bank a solid wall of lava, compelling the swift current to follow a westerly course in search of an outlet to the north. The southern bank is comparatively low, formed of sandy alluvial soil. Then the mouth of the White River is reached, that river, which comes in from the south, receiving its name from the milky color of its water. Then the stream takes a northerly course through a rugged, mountainous country, and a short distance further on the waters of Stewart River flows from the north

TRADING POST AT FORT SELKIRK

into the Yukon. At a high stage of water the current is quite swift at this point, flowing six or seven miles an hour. From Stewart River to the mouth of the Klondike both banks are closed in by high mountains, formed chiefly of basaltic rock and salty shale. Many of the bluffs are cut and worn into most picturesque shapes by glacial action. At the mouth of the Klondike above the confluence on the right bank is an Indian village, and after the river is passed there is a government reservation on the right side going down. On the left bank, or near it, is a quartz mine, belonging to Captain Healy of the North American Trading and Transportation Co, or rather to his wife.

Dawson City, the metropolis

A little lower down, on the right bank of the stream, is Dawson City, the present metropolis of the Yukon, laid out by Joseph Ladue in September, 1896, and today the liveliest frontier town on the American continent. A few miles below is Fort Reliance, which was the first place settled by whites in this region, having been used by the Hudson Bay Company as a fur trading post for several years, but afterward abandoned. There is no town there now, but the location is important because many points throughout the Yukon country were named by roughly guessing their distance above or below Fort Reliance. Thus, Sixty-Mile Creek empties into the Yukon about sixty (really fifty-three) miles above, and Forty-Mile Creek about forty (forty-eight) miles below Fort Reliance, and the stream which flows into the Yukon from the north and is marked on most of the maps "Clandindu River" is locally known as "Twelve-Mile Creek", being calculated from the same starting point. From Dawson City the course of the river is northwesterly past Fort Cudahay and Forty-Mile, where for several years there has been a considerable amount of successful placer mining carried on. The next point of importance is Circle City, where there is a post office. This town was started about five years ago and was the chief centre of mining activity on the Yukon, being the trading point for the Creek District, the most productive mining district ever worked, so far, in the United States portion of the Yukon country. For the first 100 miles after crossing the boundary the river runs in one broad stream, confined on either side by high banks and a mountainous country, known as the "Upper Ramparts." It then widens out and for 150 miles is a network of channels and small islands. At old Fort Yukon, an abandoned Hudson Bay post, the river reaches its highest northern latitude, being within the Arctic Circle. From main bank to bank the distance has been found to be seven miles, at a point just above the site of old Fort Yukon. This place is the most serious obstacle to navigation that is met with on the river from its mouth to the Five Finger Rapids near Fort Selkirk, as the channel at this point shifts from year to year, and at certain stages of the year is difficult to find.

Below Fort Yukon

Below Fort Yukon the country flattens out considerably and the majestic grandeur that one encounters from Circle City up to the headwaters is seen no more. There are occasional mountains, and some of the streams which rise in them and feed the Tanana and other tributaries of the Yukon are known to contain gold. At the mouth of the Tanana is Fort Weare, a trading station of the North American Transportation and Trading Company, and named after its president. Away from the Yukon, sixty or seventy miles northward in the Arctic Circle, are mountain streams upon which gold has been found, on the Koyukuk River and its tributaries. About ten miles

JACK MCQUESTEN'S STORE AT CIRCLE CITY
(YUKON ARCHIVES/ANCHORAGE FINE ARTS MUSEUM COLLECTION)

below the Tanana there is a quartz claim, but from there westward, there has been no gold discovered. The points on the lower river are mostly trading posts, where the trade in furs is carried on. There is a large business done with the natives in skins, and prices are regulated by the standard price of red fox or marten — called one skin — about $1.25. A prime beaver would be "two skins;" black bear, "four skins;" lynx "one skin;" land otter two or three skins, etc. Five yards drilling, or 1 lb. tea, or 1 lb. powder, or 1/2 lb. powder with 1 box caps and 1 lb. shot, are given for one skin; 50 lbs flour, four skins; 3 lbs sugar, one skin, etc. These are samples of the prices obtained by the natives, with little variation, until the mining district is reached, when the prices are higher, to conform to the prices charged to miners.

Timber and vegetation

On the lower Yukon, for many miles, the banks are devoid of timber, other than a stunted growth of willow

JACK McQUESTEN

Mr. McQuesten, who has the store at Circle City, has lived in that region for years and is a man of large heart and ready sympathy, and probably the most popular man on the Yukon.

brush, alder and cottonwood. Then spruce timber is encountered in the region of Hamilton's Landing, and from there to its headwaters the river is well supplied with spruce, fir, hemlock, birch, alder and cottonwood timber.

Spruce attains to considerable size, but it is full of knots and blemishes and makes poor lumber.

One of the most noticeable features of the vegetation of the Yukon region is the great variety of berries to be found all through the country. Among them, growing wild, and often in great profusion, are high and low bush cranberries, blueberries, salmon berries or dewberries, red currants and raspberries. The salmon berries are especially plentiful in the swampy lands of the lower Yukon, where they are gathered by the natives in large quantities.

Agricultural Possibilities

The shortness of the summer season in the interior of Alaska and the British Northwest Territory will always preclude any great amount of agricultural cultivation. Yet. as is shown by the productiveness in wild berries, the short summer season brings vegetation to maturity with great rapidity. As soon as the snow disappears in the spring there is a sudden and quick productiveness in all kinds of herbage. Isolated experiments with different kinds of vegetables have not been numerous, but they have been, to a very large extent, successful. When the sun is shining every day for twenty-four hours it accomplishes great results in a very short season. On the coast numerous successful attempts at agriculture have been made on a small scale. Potatoes have done well at all points on the river, although they do not grow to any great size; and barley has been successfully cultivated at Forty-Mile, and even at Fort Yukon, away up in the Arctic Circle. On the Stikine River in the Northwest Territory oats and wheat have also been successfully grown. The attempts at cultivation have all been made in a desultory and unscientific manner, and the people of Alaska have long desired the establishing of agricultural experimental stations by the government, both in the interior and on the coast. The expressed intention of the agricultural department to at once establish such stations, gives hope that much good will be done by intelligent experiments in crops adapted to the rigorous climate.

There are numerous plains and open spaces, not only on the coast but also in the interior, which are covered with the arctic or tundra moss, suitable for reindeer grazing, and this food is so widely and plentifully distributed as to make the introduction of reindeer to the Yukon region, now going on, a matter of great importance to the country. The interior has an abundance of nutritious grasses suitable for the feeding of domestic animals, but the winter has heretofore been found too severe to make the keeping of horses and cattle a possibility. Alaska is a great country for wild game, but during recent years the amount of game to be procured in the immediate neighbourhood of the main Yukon has steadily decreased. Up the tributary rivers, however, game is more abundant.

Fur animals of Yukon Valley

Like all countries in high latitudes, the fur-bearing animals are an especially important feature in the fauna of the Yukon region. The land otter, the brown, grizzly, silvertip and black bears, the beavers (once very common but now diminishing greatly in numbers), the beautiful silver or black fox, the red fox, cross fox, and, on the coast, the white fox, are among the most valuable of the fur animals.

The mink is common, and the Peshoo or Canadian lynx, grey and white wolves, muskrats, wolverines, rabbits, and marmots and others combine to make the list of the fur animals of the Yukon Valley very complete. Among them the brown grizzly, silver-tip and brown bears are the most formidable. Grizzly bears are only occasionally met, and the silver tip bear is not numerous. The brown bear makes its way to the mountains about the time spring opens, and fishes for salmon, a sport in which it is greatly adept. About that time the Yukon Indians are engaged in the same occupation, for drying salmon is an important industry with them. If Mr. Bear and Mr. Indian meet at this time the latter generally prefers to retire, for the brown bear is very fierce and his skin is not very valuable. The brown bear retires to the tundra or mossy plains after the fishing season. This bear, in his travels, usually finds the best travelling ground and the shallowest fords, and therefore his well trod paths become the favourite roads with travellers through the Yukon Country. The black bear is also good at fishing and is a permanent resident of the wooded and mountain regions; but is by no means to be dreaded to such an extent as his brown relative.

The Klondike River and its tributaries were at first best known to the miners of the Yukon as being infested with bears, and a general dislike to ursine society is said to have made prospecting up the Klondike unpopular. If it had not been for the bears, the Bonanza and El Dorado finds might have been made several years ago.

Moose, caribou, deer, mountain sheep, and mountain goats are found in the mountains. There are very few if any of these near the river, and one may make the entire trip up to the Klondike from Lake Lindermann without getting a chance to shoot large game.

Birds abundant on the Yukon
One of the things that will amaze the observant though unscientific new arrival on the Yukon is the great

CARIBOU HERD CROSSING RIVER
(Yukon Archives/Innes-Taylor Collection)

variety of birds he will see during the brief summer
season. The snowbirds, and winter wrens and other
winter birds of the United States live in Alaska in the
summer, and not only they but nearly all of the birds
which pass through the United States on their way
northward. Of the more than sixty species of the family of
American Warblers which are seen in the northern United
States when the cherry and apple trees are in bloom, fully
half pass on by easy stages so as to reach the Yukon
country with the warm weather. In fact this northern
region is their birthplace, and it is here, therefore, that
their nests are built, their nuptial melodies are sung and
their pretty plumage displayed. The grosbeaks, bobolinks,

and a very large number of other favourite American birds, utilize the Yukon region as a summer resort, giving beauty and melody to the surroundings. Hummingbirds are especially numerous and the brief Alaska summer brings an influx of bird species which is a delight to the ornithologist.

The bald and grey eagles, so plentiful on the Alaskan coast, are also occasionally seen in the interior. Ducks, geese, and other water fowl breed in all of the waters of the Yukon region, and in favourable places may be found in great numbers.

Fish in the Yukon

Fish are abundant — not only the salt water varieties on the coast, but also the fresh water fish of the interior. The greatest of these is salmon, which abounds on nearly all the streams, and on none to a greater extent than the Klondike, the very name of which is a mispronunciation of the Indian words "thron-dak" or "much fish".

Both hunting and fishing are, however, principally related to the Indians, as the miner, seeking to make his fortune and return to his home in the states, has little time to spare and must keep busy if he would attain his ends.

Chapter VII

Yukon Gold Country

Mining developments in Alaska and Northwest Territory

All over Alaska are mineral resources of value. Down in the southeast portion of the territory, on Douglas Island, opposite Juneau, there is located the great Treadwell mine. It is a well developed property in which the tunnels and drifts show that it is between 300 and 400 feet between the hanging wall and foot wall, the space between being quartz carrying free gold and sulphurets averaging $8 to the ton. This is low grade ore, and to make it pay it is necessary that it be worked on a large scale, with modern machinery. The extent of the deposit, assuring millions of product, justified large expenditures, and the company owning the Treadwell mine has established on Douglas Island the largest quartz mill in the world. It operates 240 stamps and never stops, night or day, summer or winter, except for repairs. There are a number of other quartz ledges in numerous places in the southeastern part of Alaska, including the Sheep Creek region, where are silver, gold and other metals; Salmon Creek, near Juneau, silver and gold; Silver Bow Basin, gold; Fuhter Bay, Admiralty Island; Silver Bay district, near Sitka, gold and silver; Besner's Bay, Lynn Canal, as well as Fish River on Norton Sound, Unga district, and Lemon Creek, all gold districts.

Little prospecting for quartz

The working of quartz mines in Alaska has practically been confined to coast localities where labour can be had

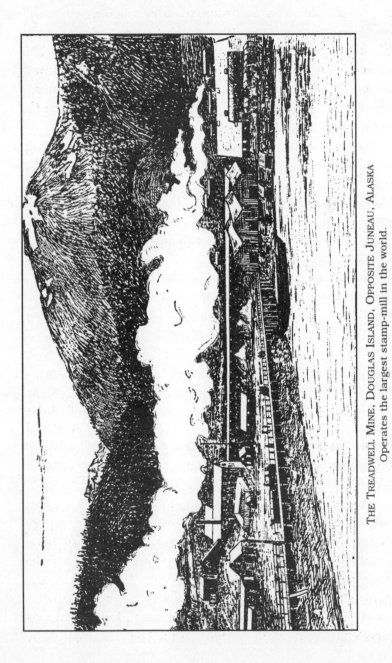

THE TREADWELL MINE, DOUGLAS ISLAND, OPPOSITE JUNEAU, ALASKA
Operates the largest stamp-mill in the world.

at reasonable rates and supplies and machinery can be procured with comparative ease. In the Yukon region there has been, so far, little prospecting for quartz. The miners who have gone there are mostly men of small means, looking for gold which they can dig themselves and wash out by means of pan or sluice box. The time for prospecting is short. Unless one has means it is necessary to find "pay dirt" which will yield at least a "grub stake" before winter, or else go to work for wages. If one should find a quartz vein it would be necessary to do the surface prospecting on the ledge before winter set in. Then, if the vein did not turn out to be very rich and the ore high grade, it would not pay to import expensive machinery at heavy freight rates and pay the present high wages.

Of course every miner expects that the largest fortunes on the Yukon, in the future, will come out of quartz mining, because where there is so much placer gold there must be a great "mother lode" somewhere, yet every man is now looking for a "poor man's mine" which requires only strength, industry and perseverance to yield either a modest or large fortune.

Outside of the Yukon region there are seven other placer districts, all located on streams flowing near the coast. The Yukon region, however, has been the centre of the Alaskan miners' hope for some years past.

The Yukon mining districts

It is an interesting fact that the first Yukon tributary to attract the attention of gold seekers was Stewart River, which is now looked upon as one of the most favourable prospecting regions. It was in 1883 that the first work was done there, and the following year brought quite a number of miners to the spot. The work done there was practically confined to the bars formed near the mouth by the spring freshets. These yielded thousands of dollars, before the discoveries at other points attracted the miners from the Stewart region. The mouth of the Stewart River is about seventy five miles above Dawson City. Its various tributaries have been little prospected prior to the present year; but doubtless many of those who have been unable to get locations on the Klondike will try the Stewart, unless the rapacity of the Canadian mining regulations should drive the bulk of the prospecting to the American tributaries of the Yukon, which may likely occur.

The Pelly River

Another stream which had something of a mining boom several years ago is the Pelly River, which also made good returns to prospectors on its bars. Little gulch mining was attempted on the creeks and streamlets emptying into the Pelly, but the entire region of the Yukon from Teslin Lake to the Tanana is known to be auriferous.

Sixty-Mile Creek

Sixty-Mile Creek and its tributaries Miller and Glacier Creeks are streams in which a considerable amount of mining has been done, although the settlement at Sixty-Mile Post which is on an island at the mouth of Sixty-Mile Creek never became very large. Its principal industry was the cutting of lumber to be rafted down to the more important camps below, the small stream sawmill being owned by Joseph Ladue, now widely famous as the owner of Dawson City. The logs are rafted down stream to the mill from the timbered regions near and below Fort Selkirk.

Forty-Mile

Forty-Mile was long the chief town of the Upper Yukon. In the old Hudson's Bay trading days, when furs rather

SIXTY-MILE, YUKON RIVER

than gold were the magnet that drew white men to the Yukon, all the streams that were named at all were designated as so many miles from the trading post at Fort Reliance. In 1888 the number of miners on Forty-Mile Creek and its tributaries became sufficiently great to cause the Alaska Commercial Company to establish on the east side of the mouth of the creek their station, called after the river "Forty-Mile", placing it in charge of Mr. Jack McQuesten, who is known to everybody in the Yukon valley and who conducts stores both at Forty-Mile and Circle City.

STORE AT FORTY-MILE

INDIAN VILLAGE ON FORTY-MILE CREEK, YUKON RIVER

Fort Cudahy

Westward of the creek about three quarters of a mile and fronting on the Yukon is the station of the North American Transportation and Trading Company, known as Fort Cudahy, so named after Mr. John Cudahy, the well known Chicago packer, who is a director of the company.

Forty-Mile and its tributaries have been mined with a considerable degree of success for ten years, but the town lost some of its population about 1893 in the rush to the Birch Creek mines. Even since that it has remained an important point, although it has been almost depopulated by the recent rush to the Klondike. The valuable mines of the Forty-Mile district will continue to be worked, however, and the stations at the mouth of the creek remain important supply points.

Circle City and Birch Creek district

Circle City is the recently dethroned metropolis of the Yukon mining regions. It gained its prominence in 1893,

FORT CUDAHY, 1895

One of several settlements downstream from Dawson City.

when the richness of the Birch Creek region became known. It is not, like the other stations on the Upper Yukon, at the mouth of a tributary stream. The mouth of Birch Creek is about two hundred and twenty miles below Circle City, its course being almost parellel with the Yukon.

RAFTING THROUGH THE ICE ON THE YUKON

At Circle City the portage from the Yukon to Birch Creek is only eight miles, so that Circle City is the trading point for the Birch Creek Mining District, and both the Alaska Commercial Company and the North American Transportation and Trading Company have stores located here. The eight miles of portage for goods from the town to the Creek makes the cost of provisions very high in the Birch Creek mining camps. There are a few horses at Circle City which pack provisions to the camps forty to seventy miles away, but the carriage costs $45 per 100 lbs. for the greater distance. Some miners carry their goods or have them packed over by Indians the eight miles to Birch Creek. But if this is done one has to pole up stream for from forty to seventy miles, making several portages around rapids. and at the head of canoe navigation to carry the provisions several miles up the particular tributary upon which the claim he is working is located. There are several of these tributaries, of which Mastodon, Molymute and Eagle Creek have turned out a very large amount of gold, and several good claims have also been partly worked on Boulder, Independence, Greenhord, Deadwood, Mammoth, and Harrison Creeks.

The Birch Creek District is the most important, so far developed, on the United States side of the Alaska boundary. The Forty-Mile Creek district is partly on the United States side and partly in Canadian territory, the creek emptying into the Yukon on the British side.

White River

The headwaters of White River are somewhere in the Mt. Elias group of mountains, and the meager reports of those who have been over the ground indicate that these headwaters and tributaries are gold bearing. The best road to that region is by the Burton's trail route over Chilkat Pass, but it has been little travelled, and no one except experienced mountaineers who go in a party with a first-class equipment should attempt to make the trip. Going up White River from its mouth is also a troublesome journey, as the current is very swift.

Tanana River

The Tanana River, which enters the Yukon at Weare, is another very large stream, wholly in American territory, which will doubtless attract the attention of explorers. Some few parties have made excursions up that river, but the natives are said to be somewhat ill disposed toward white intrusion, and the exploration should be well organized to be successful. A few bars on the lower banks of the Tanana have been worked, and have produced gold in paying quantities.

The Koyukuk River and its tributaries have also been prospected with good results. Speaking in general terms, it may be said that all of the streams entering the Lewis and Yukon Rivers, from the Hootalinqua down to Hamilton's Landing, show evidence of gold in paying quantities being distributed throughout the interior of Alaska. It is not too much to claim that Alaska, so far as present knowledge exists, has more extensive and richer placer deposits than any other section of the world, and those who know the country best will be greatly disappointed if the output of the Yukon mines during the next ten years does not exceed that of California in its palmiest days.

The Klondike district

The latest discoveries in placer mines in the Yukon region have set the continent in a flame of excitement. Not only those to whom the digging of gold from the ground has an aspect of romance and unreality, but also those whose knowledge of mines is practical and intimate, are so overwhelmed by the tangible and indisputable evidence as to admit that nothing in the history of mining has ever equalled the events on the Klondike during the past year. My own acquaintance with mining covers a third of a century, beginning with a toilsome and perilous trip to the Echuca diggings in Australia in 1864, but after all these years, during which I have been in many mining districts all over the world, I am free to confess that the Klondike discoveries outclass all of the great gold strikes I ever knew or heard of. The narrative of the finding of gold on

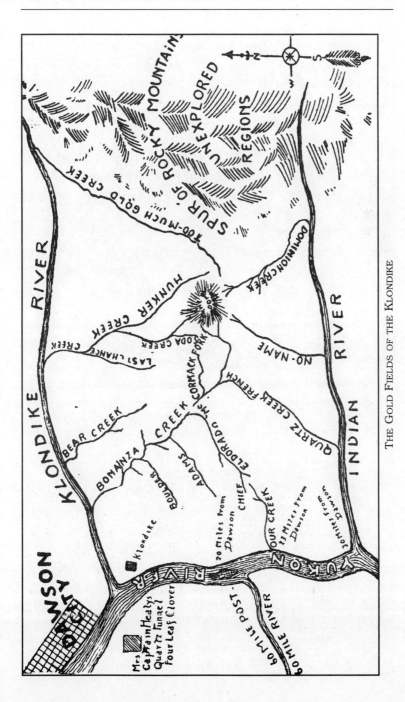

The Gold Fields of the Klondike

PROSPECTING ON ONE OF THE TRIBUTARIES OF THE KLONDIKE

Bonanza and El Dorado Creeks has been already told, up
to the time that the returning miners brought news of the
great discoveries that had been made. It now remains to
describe the mines in what is popularly known as the
"Klondike District". It may be well to say, however, that
there are no mines on the Klondike, so far as known. That
river is too large and deep to be worked as a placer mine.
There may be and probably are, bars on the main river
that will yield fine gold, but the great mines of which we
hear so much are on the tributaries of that stream. The
Bonanza and its tributaries, especially the El Dorado, are
known to be of surpassing richness. Estimates placed
upon individual claims by their owners have been given
and much tangible proof offered, but the statements of
Mr. William Ogilvie, Dominion Surveyor in charge of the

boundary survey, are, if anything, still more astounding. In an official report from Dawson City in regard to the district, he says: "The extent of the gold-bearing section here is such as to warrant the assertion that we have here a district which will give 1,000 claims of 500 feet in length each. Now 1,000 such claims will require at least 3,000 men to work them properly, and as wages for working in the mines are from $8 to $10 a day, without board, we have every reason to assume that this part of our territory will within a year or two contain 10,000 souls at least, for the news has gone out to the coast and an unprecedented influx is expected next spring. And this is not all, for a large creek called Indian Creek joins the Yukon River about midway between Klondike and the Stewart River, and all along this creek good pay dirt has been found. All that has stood in the way of working it herefore has been the scarcity of provisions and the difficulty of getting them up there even when here. Indian Creek is quite a large stream, and it is probable it will yield 500 or 600 claims. Further south yet lies the head of the several branches of the Stewart River, on which some prospecting has been done this summer and good indications found, but the want of provisions prevented development.

"Since my last the prospects on Bonanza Creek and tributaries are increasing in richness and extent, until now it is certain millions will be taken out of the district in the next few years. On some of the claims prospected the pay dirt is of great extent and very rich. One man told me yesterday that he washed out a single pan of dirt on one of the claims on Bonanza Creek and found $14.25 in it. Of course, that may be an exceptionally rich pan, but $5 to $7 per pan is the average on that claim, it is reported, with five feet pay dirt and the width yet undetermined, but known to be thirty feet; even at that figure the result at nine to ten pans to the cubic foot, and 500 feet long, is $4,000,000 at $5 per pan. One fourth of this would be enormous. Enough prospecting has been done to show that there are at least fifteen miles of this extraordinary richness, and the indications are that we will have three or four times that extent, if not all equal to the above, at least very rich."

Since this report was written there have been a large number of other creeks and branches located, including a number of gulches tributary to Hunker Creek, and its branch, Gold Bottom Creek. Indian Creek or River, which flows into the Yukon from the east, thirty miles above Dawson, has also been located, its tributaries, including Quartz Creek and Dominion Creek, both having had their discovery claims located in June of the present year.

The Indians have claimed that further up the Klondike than Hunker Creek there was a creek where there was "too much gold", meaning that it was richer than the Bonanza or El Dorado. About thirty-eight miles from the mouth of the Klondike a creek has been found which its discoverers have named "Too Much Gold Creek", and this has also been taken up in claims. Of course it may turn out that these other creeks may not prove to be profitable, but so far as heard from all of them prospect well, and every report that comes tends to increase the probability of rich returns from this famous district.

The Klondike River, which heads in the Rocky mountains, is said to be about one hundred and fifty miles long, and is a bold and rapid stream. Bonanza Creek empties into the Klondike about one and one-half miles up from the mouth. It is twenty-five miles long, and heads at the Dome, a large, bold mountain, in which a number of small creeks have their source. El Dorado, which is seven miles long, is a tributary of Bonanza, the

CAMPING ON THE KLONDIKE

confluence being twelve miles above the mouth of the latter stream. The latest reports show that the "pay" on Bonanza is good from the 60s below the point of discovery, where one claim has 20 and 25 cent dirt, with the pay 125 feet wide, up to forty-three above, claim No. 41 being very rich. Gold on Bonanza is finer than that on El Dorado. There is not a blank up to No.38, and there are some good claims above that number. The richest claims are in the middle of the gulch, the gold there being coarse, with lots of nuggets. This, with the fractions of claims, makes nearly twenty miles of paying ground.

In addition there are a number of side gulches on which good prospects have been discovered. Bonanza district, it is estimated, is likely to produce not less than $50,000,000 in gold, and this is believed to be an under estimate than otherwise. Hunker Creek empties into the Klondike twelve miles up and is twenty miles long. In places $2 and $3 to the pan on bedrock have been found, and the indications are that it will prove a rich-paying creek. Gold Bottom, a fork, and Last Chance, a side gulch, show up equally well for a considerable distance. These comprise, with Bear Creek, which comes into the

Klondike between Bonanza and Hunker, the extent of territory of which anything certain is known. Quartz Creek and Indian Creek are reached from the heads of Bonanza and Hunker and they have also some prospects. The country rock is slate and mica schist. Many of the nuggets are full of quartz. Iron rock is found with them, and pieces of stratified rock containing iron are found showing plainly on their sides the matrices of gold nuggets. Some fair gold-bearing quartz has been discovered, but no rich, free gold-bearing rock in place. The mineral belt seems to run northeast and southwest, if one may judge from the creeks, and to be about ten miles wide. It seems to parallel the main range of mountains about 100 miles distant from it.

Chapter VIII

How To Get There

Who should go and how they must outfit and travel

While there is no question that vast riches are in the ground in the Yukon country, it must be remembered that this wealth can only be procured at the end of a long, tedious journey, that the steamboat route by St. Michaels and up the Yukon is only practicable for about ten weeks of the year; that the usual overland route is beset by dangers which may well appall any but the stoutest hearts, and will tax even the strongest and sturdiest constitutions, and that dangers with strong chances of death are ever present over a considerable portion of the trip.

It should further be remembered that in the great multitude of gold seekers who are flocking to the Yukon disappointment must come to many. There is a very large element of chance in all placer mining, and even in the richest mining districts the blanks are many.

At the end of the journey, even under the best circumstances, are many discomforts. For nine months the community, whether it numbers three thousand or thirty thousand, will be absolutely cut off from every source of food supply, except that which it has in its own hands, and the provisions on hand in September will have to last until June. If the supply is adequate, the danger will be reduced to a minimum, but if it falls short starvation — or at least great privation — must come to many.

The great rush which has been made will severely tax the meager capacity of the two trading companies to supply. Those who go should be prepared with a year's provisions, at least.

Those who go should remember that placer mining,

especially on the Yukon, is very hard labour. How hard will be explained in another part of this book. It consists of hard, continuous digging in frozen ground for the greater part of the year, and equally hard work shovelling, panning, etc., during the remaining months. The only variation from this is intervals of house building, carrying wood for fuel, cooking, etc.

If you are a professional man your training will do you no good. An ounce of physical culture is worth ten pounds of classical or scientific training so far as placer mining is concerned. A knowledge of carpentering will come handy for one's personal benefit, but not as a means of employment, for nearly every man who goes there will build his own house. Other mechanical trades will avail little except as they have trained the muscle.

AT CIRCLE CITY

Experienced miner has slight advantage

On the other hand the experienced miner has only a slight advantage. It is of course true that experience is a good thing in mining as in other avocations, and in quartz mining is an absolute necessity, but the whole history of placer mining is full of illustrations of the fact that the

MINING IS HARD WORK
A trio of miners demonstrate some of the more difficult and dangerous
work that awaits those who seek gold.

(Yukon Archives/D. Bohn Collection)

novice — the "tenderfoot" as they say in the west, or the "new chum", as he used to be called in the Australian mines — is just as likely to find the richest pay as is the old and grizzled prospector who has been in the forefront of every gold rush from Hangtown to Klondike. The experienced miner, other things being equal, will get at results somewhat quicker than the raw hand, but then there is no avocation in which experience comes quicker, or in more solid chunks, than in placer mining.

The requisites, then, are a sound body, a strong and willing arm, and a brave heart. Add to these industry and perseverance, temperance and a cool head, and a man is well equipped for the journey and the life at the end.

The weaklings, the timid, the easily discouraged and roysterers would do well to stay at home. In such a climate as the Klondike, with the conditions of life that are there, only the fittest will survive the inevitable struggle with the forces of nature.

Go prepared

One should go there prepared to fight it out with fortune for two, three or five years. Some women have gone there and stood the ordeal as well as men, but unless at the call of duty, as a helpmate to a husband, or something out of the ordinary way, it is better for a woman to stay away.

Those who go for pleasure will find that they have gone to the wrong place. Life on the Yukon is a hard experience at the very best.

The trip by sea

If the gold seeker goes by either of the transportation lines to St. Michaels and thence up the Yukon he will save himself many inconveniences. It is not an unpleasant trip, unless one is seasick, and the dangers are only those of navigation, which are not many. Going by this route, the ordinary fare from Seattle or San Francisco is $150. One is allowed to carry free 150 pounds of baggage, but no provisions. The companies will, however, agree to furnish one with provisions for one year for $400. Therefore for $550, plus the fare to Seattle or San Francisco, one may be relieved from the difficulties about getting to the Klondike and food after he arrives.

Yet there is an outfit to get. One cannot go so far toward the North Pole without clothes — very heavy clothing for winter. What is needed will be discussed when we get to the overland journey. If one goes on the early boat so as to get there when navigation opens he will need summer as well as winter clothes. It is quite warm up there for two months.

No place for starched shirts

There are many things one can just was well leave behind — starched shirts, for instance and all kinds of gewgaws. The summer season is short, but the daylight is continuous. If we are going to mine we must first find our claim. How we go about it will be explained later. When it is found we have to work on it sufficiently to see if it will justify us in putting in our winter's work on it. If so, we have a house to build and to make tight and warm for winter, wood to bring and a lot more of very hard work which only calls for working clothes.

Winter apparel

For winter the nearer we approach the Siwash or the Eskimo in our outside apparel the better off we will be. In making preparations, therefore, use and not appearance should be the controlling consideration.

After leaving Seattle, San Francisco or Portland a

straight shoot is made for Dutch Harbour, on the island of Unalaska. This island is the most important of the Aleutian chain, and was the earliest seat of Russian dominion in Northwest America. The island is mountainous and the higher eminences are snow capped, but below the snowline everything is of a beautiful green appearance. Dutch Harbour is on an island in an enclosed bay, and here there is a supply station of the company which owns the sealing privilege of the Pribilof Islands, as well as of the steamship companies engaged in Yukon trade, and the fleets of whaling vessels also use the harbour as a base of supplies. This place, about 2,000 miles from Seattle, is the first stop made by the steamer. The stop is very brief and the journey is then renewed northward through Bering Sea to St. Michaels Island. You will notice by the map that you have passed the mouth of the Yukon about sixty miles, but this seems to be unavoidable, because the delta lands of the Yukon are so badly overflowed during the high waters of the first half of the navigation season that no suitable place for a station can be found at any point nearer than St. Michaels. It was known as Michaelovsky in the days of Russian domination, and was founded by the Russians in 1835. They were cordially welcomed at that time by the natives, the Mahlemoots, who had two villages known respectively as Taheik and Agahbak, near which the Russians built a fort. The two native villages were depopulated by smallpox in 1842.

Description of St. Michaels

The town is an irregularly built collection of old Russian buildings mixed in with the warehouses of the companies doing business on the river, and those of some independent traders. Altogether the white population numbers about fifty, and there are also several hundred

Innuits or Eskimos who are resident upon the island. The island is treeless, but is quite green during the summer season, and its rolling surface reminds one of some of the prairie regions of the western states. Across the narrow estuary rise several conical hills, formerly volcanoes. It does not get so cold at St. Michaels as in the interior. The average temperature, according to observation, is as follows:

January	-5°	May	32.8°	September	43.3°
February	6°	June	45.2°	October	28.0°
March	9.5°	July	53.1°	November	18.3°
April	22.1°	August	52.1°	December	8.9°

The season of regular snowfall begins at St. Michaels about October 1, and by October 20 ice has formed at the mouth of the Yukon. Navigation ends before October, however, because the freeze begins earlier on the upper river, and the mouth is closed tight by about the first of November and remains fast sealed until about the fifth of June, when the ice begins to break up. In ten days more the river is again clear for navigation. The sea about St. Michaels is usually covered by sludgy floes as early as the middle or end of October, and these open and close irregularly until the next June.

Fort Get There

Near the town proper is the station of the North American Transportation and Trading Company, to which they have given the distinctively American name of "Fort Get There".

When you get to St. Michaels you will perhaps find a boat waiting to take you along up the Yukon. Perhaps you will have to wait for it. When it comes you will get aboard

(Yukon Archives / Coutts Collection)

ST. MICHAELS

and start back southward until the mouth of the Yukon is reached. Then the trip is made up the river, at first through a flat country, then through one interspersed with mountains. There are Indian villages here and there along the lower river, where all the inhabitants seem to be engaged in drying salmon. When you first get on board your Yukon steamer you think you will like some of this fish. They gratify you on board by giving you plenty of it. Next meal, more salmon, and so on until you are salmon hungry no more. However, you will fare well on these steamers, considering the distance you are from civilization. In the general description of the Yukon region we have told you of the places you will pass on the river. In the stretch between Weare, at the mouth of the Tanana, and Circle City, you are surprised at the vast number of islands, large and small, that dot the stream, which is through this long distance very wide — at some points as much as seven miles. You begin to wonder how many of these islands there are, until somebody suggests forty or fifty thousand. You are willing to let it go at that, and then fall to wondering how the captain or pilot, or whoever it is that has charge of the steering directions, can ever find the somewhat uncertain and somewhat shifting channel. That is, you do these things, and some others, if you are coming up late in the season. If you are on the first boat that comes up in June you do not have time for anything trivial. The one serious business in life is fighting mosquitoes, gnats and their kindred, and listening to the yarns of the old time Yukoner (whom you would just then like to strangle), as he tells you how much worse they are higher up, where, he informs you, "you have to chop your way through'em with an axe." This is one of the things you have to endure, in summer, on the Yukon.

Above Circle City you will have some magnificent mountain scenery to admire, grand upheavals that are sublime in their rugged beauty. When you get to Dawson you will congratulate yourself upon having reached it without trouble.

That is, of course, if you get there. If one does not leave Seattle until the last steamer it is quite possible that he will have to spend the winter at some place en route. The company can not, and will not, guarantee to get their passengers to Dawson City so late in the season, although they try, of course, to do so, and time the steamers' departure with that end in view. But any misadventure causing delay, or an early winter season, will prevent them from making the trip through. Doubtless the companies will increase their carrying capacity by the summer of 1898.

Clothing for the trip and mines

Some of the things that one needs in making the overland journey will not be required if the trip is made by sea, and if one has arranged his food supply with the transportation company of course the load will be lightened.

However one goes, however, he will require a good outfit of clothing, all of the useful order. Two suits of stout clothing such as corduroy or the stoutest jeans, or one jacket and two pairs of pants; about three pairs of heavy wool socks and three of ordinary socks; two pairs of blanket lined mittens; two pairs of rubber boots and a can of rubber cement to repair them with if they crack; two or three pairs of shoes, both stout and one pair extra heavy, five or six yards of mosquito netting of the best quality; one or two caps; sou'wester cap, rubber coat for summer; three suits heavy underwear; three or four heavy woollen shirts, a sweater, two summer negligee shirts, two rough towels, and a cartridge belt.

Steamboat landing at Dawson City

Take along a bachelors sewing outfit, needles, thread pair of scissors, piece of beeswax, shirt buttons, hand snap, trousers buttons, etc.

You will want a shaving outfit. You may think you do not, but if you ever have your beard frozen into a solid icicle you will change your mind.

For the more severe winter weather fur garments are desirable, in fact essential for comfort. These can be bought in Juneau if the demand has not swamped the supply. There are winter boots, made of seal and walrus skins, and winter or dry weather boots made of various kinds of furs. Trousers are made of various kinds of skin, principally that of the marmot, or Siberian ground squirrel.

The Yukon Miner's Parka

A most important and characteristic garment is the "parka", or upper garment made of marmot and muskrat skins or tanned reindeer hides, with enormous winter hoods or collars of dog hair, fox fur or still better, trimmed with the long hair of the wolverine or glutton. This "parka" has sleeves and compasses the body of the wearer without an opening before or behind from his neck to his feet. His head is thrust through an aperture left for it; and it has a puckering string which draws it snugly around the neck. This is a favorite and in fact universal winter garment with the Inuuits or Eskimos of the coast, the most esteemed kind being made of alder-bark-tanned reindeer skin for winter use, with the hair worn inside. The wolverine trimming of the hood is much favoured by white residents of the Yukon country, the hair, which is five or six inches long, being useful in protecting the face without obscuring the vision. A well made parka will cost from $25 to $100 according to the material, but it is practically cold-proof. Less expensive fur garments can be procured,

KLONDIKE MINER IN WINTER ATTIRE

but will not afford as much protection as the native garment.

Besides the blankets, fur robes will be found very acceptable as a part of the winter bedding outfit. The Chilkat blankets of goat wool used to be famous, but those that the Chilkat Indians sell today are for the greater part base imitations.

Of course, not every one who goes to the Yukon will have the same outfit of clothing, but all should go prepared for an arctic winter.

Do not forget a pair of snow glasses, made of blue or green glass, which will prevent against snow blindness.

Oilskin bags, to hold provisions likely to be injured by water, are also very useful.

A fur lined canvas sleeping bag is a most valuable addition to the outfit.

Tools, utensils and outfit

Those going by the overland route will need not only a miner's, but also a woodsman's, boatman's and boatbuilder's outfit. These can be made as extensive as desired, but it should be remembered that they all have to be carried, either by their owner or by Indians at ruinous rates.

A large whip saw, small hand saw, draw knife, pocket knife, pocket rule, small hunting knife, hatchet, chisel, axe, about six pounds of assorted nails (wire nails two and four inches long are most needed), brace and bit, five pounds of pitch, three pounds oakum, a caulking iron, and about fifty feet of 5/8 inch rope and some sail canvas is about the minimum outfit. If the party consists of three or four a few more tools, such as a jack plane and an additional saw or hatchet will be found useful. So might an adze, but as before stated, economy in weight is a very important feature where portages over steep trails have to be made, even after the Chilkoot Pass has been scaled.

Camp equipage

The camp equipage should consist of a tent (the size of which should be accommodated to that of the party, but it should be snug), a frying pan, baking pan, granite kettle, bread pan, coffee pot, granite plate and cup, large mixing spoon, and a knife, fork and spoon for each of the party. A small sheet iron stove with three telescopic lengths of pipe should be included in the outfit. Fishing tackle (trout line and hooks) will pay for the taking.

A pick, shovel and pan will do to start with as far as prospecting is concerned.

A good Winchester rifle with reloading tools and a hundred rounds of ammunition, with a cartridge belt, is a very useful part of the outfit. Game is not very plentiful along the main traveled route, but an occasional shot at fresh meat may be procured. When the journey's end is reached the rifle will help out the larder to a considerable extent.

Provisions for a year

The greatest of all dangers to the man who ventures into the Yukon mining regions is that he may find the food supply scarce. Even if he has money he may not be able to buy enough to eat. The amount of food getting into the district before everything freezes up limits the supply until the next June. If many go in without food supplies they will have to depend upon buying at exorbitant rates, and if the stock is exhausted before summer comes they will have to go without. The only safe way is to take a year's supply of food along. This will, of course, vary with the individual, but the appetite is sure to be good, and the stock should be something like this:

500 lbs flour, 100 lbs. corn meal, 50 lbs. oatmeal, 150 lbs. beans, 25 lbs. coffee, 12 lbs. tea, 10 lbs. salt, 75 lbs. sugar, 100 lbs. assorted evaporated fruits, good supply of evaporated vegetables, 40 lbs. dessicated potatoes, 150 lbs. bacon, 10 lbs. dried beef, 1/2 lb pepper, 10 lbs. baking powder. Other things may be added such as condensed milk, etc., to suit the individual taste and pocket, always remembering that it is a requisite to economize weight as much as possible.

A pound of citric acid should be included in the outfit. It is not only a pleasant drink, but is also a preventive

PROVISIONS ON THE BEACH AT DYEA, ALASKA

Provisions were the key to survival, and a minimum of one ton per person was required to enter Canada.

(Yukon Archives/Bill Roozeboom Collection)

against the scurvy, which is the complaint most prevalent on the Yukon. Other things that should be taken are medicines of a simple character.

Above all, do not forget matches. They should be kept in a can or oil sack, and should not be packed so tight as to make the ignition of the whole supply at once a possibility.

You now have quite a load, but one should not go without a full supply. You should have some money in your purse; not only enough to pay your way, but also enough to last some time after you get to the end of your journey. It will cost something — and a considerable amount too — to get you and your supplies up to the Klondike.

Chapter IX

The Juneau Routes

How to go down the Yukon from its headwaters

In a former part of this book the Yukon River region has been described in a general way. It was there stated that the Yukon is formed by the junction of the Lewis and Pelly Rivers.

The most common method of reaching the mines is by the Juneau route. Either from San Francisco or Seattle, one can go by steamer to Juneau, which is the largest city in Alaska — or was until Dawson City attained its recent prominence.

The time for starting

There are parties going over this route all months of the year from March to September. If a party goes over before the snow melts in the mountains they can haul their supplies much more easily by the use of sleds. The sled used for this purpose should not be more than seven or eight inches high, seven and a half feet long and about one foot four inches in width. The runners should be metal shod, brass being the best material for this purpose. Sleds can generally be used until the middle of April. After that the snow begins to melt and the expense and toil of getting the outfit to the headwaters of the Yukon are greatly increased.

Some go earlier in the year and use dog-sleds, but the cold that must be encountered is terrific and no person who is not experienced in arctic travel should undertake it.

When snowstorms are encountered

It should always be remembered, too, that those going either too early or too late are likely to encounter snowstorms of such severity that they often overwhelm the traveller. Many a person has perished in those storms before being able to reach shelter.

Juneau is situated on the mainland, on a narrow strip of nearly level ground between the sea and a lofty, snowcapped mountain, rising 3,300 feet above. It was founded in 1880, at which time Joseph Juneau and Richard Harris prospected in the neighbourhood. They found gold in the ravines and gorges of Gold Creek, where the settlement which the miners first called Harrisburg, after Richard Harris, then Rockwell, after a United States navel officer, and finally by resolution of a miners' meeting settled on the name "Juneau".

Joseph Juneau was a nephew of Soloman Juneau, who was the founder of the city of Milwaukee, Wis., a fact which the latter city has duly commemorated by the erection of a statue in honour of the latter.

Juneau without legal existence

As the government has not yet extended the land laws to Alaska, Juneau, although a city of over two thousand inhabitants, has no legal existence, and the only title of its inhabitants is that of "squatter sovereignty.". Yet they are very enterprising, have a good water works system and electric light plant, and are supporters of two or three newspapers.

From Juneau the route lies up the Lynn Canal, which has two inlets, known respectively as the Chilkat and Chilkoot inlets, leading up to the passes of the same names.

The *Chilkat Pass route* is not well known. It is known as the "Dalton Trail", from the fact that Mr. Jack Dalton and a number of Indians in his employ passed over the route a few years ago. It is said that a native in Mr. Dalton's employ passed over the trail afoot and reached the Yukon River, just above Fort Selkirk, in fourteen days.

The White Pass Route

The White Pass route is being developed by the British Yukon Company, who have constructed over it a rough pack trail. The Canadian government is being urged to build over the pass a wagon road, preliminary to the construction of a railway. The summit of this pass is 2,600 feet above the sea, and it is said that a little work would make it much superior to the Chilkoot route. The idea is to use the new route as a pack trail, with a saving in expense and toil in reaching Lake Tagish, or by taking another direction which presents few difficulties, to reach Lake Teslin, which is at the head of the Hootalinqua River. There the boat can be built and the trip down to Dawson can be made with little difficulty, eliminating the dangers of White Horse Rapids and Miles Cañon[1]. The only bad place on the route would be the Five Finger Rapids, which are by no means so dangerous as the other two.

Recent reports are that several parties have their outfits packed over that route, but it will take some work on the part of the company having it in charge before the prospecting parties will abandon the well-worn Chilkoot route.

To reach the White Pass route as well as Chilkoot Pass it is necessary to go to Dyea, sometimes spelled "Ty-a".

The town of Dyea

From Juneau to Dyea, eight[2] miles, we take the little steamer "Rustler". There are others, now that the road is

(1) Today, the spelling is "Miles Canyon".
(2) Although the original text states this, it is likely a typographical error, as the distance is closer to eighty miles.

HEALY AND WILSON'S TRADING POST
A popular meeting place at Dyea.
(Yukon Archives/Alaska Historical Library Collection)

crowded, but the "Rustler" has taken so many safely that
it seems to be part of the route itself. When reached, Dyea
proves to be an Indian village and trading post up a creek
of the same name. The village has been there a long while,
but the trading post was established later by Captain J.J.
Healy, now general manager of the North American
Transportation and Trading Company. The place is
marked "Healy's store" on many of the maps. There are
several stores there now, and the last chance to procure
supplies for several hundred miles is presented here.

From Dyea six miles further can be made by canoes and then we disembark.

Over Chilkoot Pass

From Dyea we can make arrangements with the Chilkoot Indians to pack all of our outfit to Lake Lindermann, about twenty-seven miles distant over the pass. The established packing rate heretofore has been from twelve to fifteen cents a pound. This makes the expense very heavy, but the only other alternative is to carry the load ourselves. This is obviously impossible, unless we make many trips backward and forward. This is sometimes done, but it means possibly weeks of toil and exposure.

From the head of canoe navigation we go through the canyon, up a steep ascent, to Sheep Camp. Sometimes it is possible to have supplies packed on horses to this point, and in winter pack horses can be used to within half a mile of the summit of Chilkoot Pass. At this time the further progress by sleds can be continued for a long distance; but after the snow has melted off the lower levels the route is impassable for animals.

After resting at Sheep Camp, where we have made camp for the night, we start at daybreak, following the trail up the canyon until we reach the overhanging rocks which, affording shelter from storms, have received the name of Stone House. The summit is two miles above, by a precipitous and circuitous route. It must be crossed in good weather, and if a storm is brewing there is nothing else to do except to camp at Stone House and wait. The larger number of those making the trip rest here.

The tug of war

Now comes the tug of war. The first mile and a half is bad enough, but the last half mile is true Alpine work. If you are carrying a load, so much the harder. The 2,400 foot

TRAIL ALONG DYEA RIVER

A family, carrying heavy packs and pulling a hand cart, starting out.

(Yukon Archives/Winter and Pond Collection)

Bridge spanning unfrozen section of the Dyea River
Photographer Lloyd V. Winter is assisted by two local Indians.

TRAIL ALONG DYEA CANYON, 1987
Men and a woman hauling sleds along snow-covered trail.

(Yukon Archives / Winter and Pond Collection)

ON THE ROAD TO THE KLONDIKE – AT SHEEP CAMP

MINERS AT SHEEP CAMP

climb from Stone House to the summit, through the snow,
or in the summer through a mixture of slush and rocks,
is about the hardest physical exertion we shall meet on
our trip. We reach the top well winded, tired and relieved.
If we have been carrying a heavy pack we lay it down and
take a rest. On our way up we have passed two or three
noteworthy glaciers — one a short distance above Sheep
Camp, and the other as we near the summit, a wall of
blue ice towering a thousand feet above the pass. We are
not going to meet such another piece of road, unless we
are trying to do our own packing. If this is the case we
must go back and bring up the goods we have left behind.

It is often necessary, in making journeys in this
country, to *cache* part of our outfit, that is to say, to put it
in a place where it is covered up so that animals will not
devour it. Over in the timbered regions this is often done
by building a receptacle of logs, mounted on uprights,
high above the groundling vermin and bear-tight. Articles
so *cached* are almost invariably respected, both by whites
and Indians, he who would do violence to a cache being
looked upon, by Yukoners, in about the same light that a
horse thief is regarded in western Texas.

We will assume, however, that in the present case the
packing has been hired out to the Chilkats as far as Lake
Lindermann, or at least all except the amount the
members of the party can themselves carry in a single trip.

The descent to Lake Lindermann

If there is snow all the way the nine-mile down-hill trip
to Lake Lindermann is quite easy. From the summit the
first descent is about six hundred feet to Crater Lake, the
top of what was once a volcano but is now a lake about a
mile wide. It is the actual source of the great Yukon, a
river which at its mouth, about 2,200 miles below,

ON THE WAY TO THE KLONDIKE
Miners and Indians packing outfit up the steep ascent
above Stone House, Chilkoot Pass

AT STONE HOUSE, CHILKOOT PASS

discharges into Norton Sound a larger volume of water than is emptied into the Mexican Gulf by the Mississippi.

There are two or three other small lakes to be skirted and some shallow but swift rivulets to be waded, before we reach Lake Lindermann. Here we make a camp, because we have a raft to build, and we are tired out. There is a difference of many degrees of temperature between this lake and the summit of Chilkoot Pass, but it is still cold enough, even here, except during the period from June to September.

Down the Lake Chain

Our journey now lies through a chain of connected lakes which culminate in that arm of the Yukon known as Lewis River. When we get to the shore of Lake Lindermann, we find timber plentiful, but small. It is best to build a raft here, because the timber to build boats is scarce, and there is a portage to be made at the other end of this lake.

A CACHE IN THE YUKON

PARTY OF MINERS AND INDIANS ON THE SUMMIT AT CHILKOOT PASS

At the first camp we make on Lake Lindermann the Indians keep us company until morning. They bid us goodbye after trying to borrow a little tobacco from those of our party who use it, and then we begin, as soon as we have breakfasted, to get logs together for our raft. After enough material has been gathered, we anchor out the largest and longest log, then float out another large log and lash it alongside, and so on until we have it wide enough. Then we make another layer crosswise, then another across that, and then a fourth, and then light poles, until we can put our goods on top of the raft and have them well out of the water. The raft should be well calculated in this regard, for it may be well above water at the start, but with a ton or so of freight and several hundred pounds of fortune hunters, the entire contrivance is likely to be under water, to the great detriment of many of our belongings — sugar and salt, for instance. We are glad we thought of the oil bags.

The logs should be all procured and piled up before the raft is made, and the structure should be put together as quickly as possible, because as the logs get water-soaked they sink deeper into the lake. When we are ready we pole out into the lake, hoist a sail if we have one, and without hugging the shore too closely we keep toward the right bank until we see a well worn trail. Then we take our raft to the shore, unload it, and make a portage of less than half a mile across to Lake Bennett. A crooked river, a mile long, connects the two lakes; but it consists of rapids and rugged rocks, and we do not care to risk our belongings.

Lumber at $100 per thousand

A year or two ago a party of men brought over the pass, in the early spring when the sledding was good, a small boiler, engine and circular saw. They were going to build a boat, put the engine and boiler into it for motive power, and go down the river. By the time their mill was up and in running order, along came a party of prospectors and wanted to buy lumber of them. Since then they have been kept busy selling lumber at $100 per thousand, or ready-built boats for from $75 upward. They have not been able to supply the demand which the new rush has brought upon them. Many have to cut out their lumber with the whipsaw in order to make their boats, timber being quite plentiful.

It will take about six hundred feet of lumber to make a boat to hold four men and outfits. It will be from twenty five to thirty feet long, and should be carefully and strongly made. Boats for the Yukon are made in all styles, and some without any style at all. The best are made with lap streaks, and are tightly caulked with oakum and pitch. Take enough time to make the boat a sound one, for it must last a considerable time and withstand rough usage.

When the raft is completed and loaded, the voyage is commenced. A good sail will help immensely, and if your party are not sufficiently adept to make a sloop rig for the boat, a square sail will do very well.

Keep to the right

The right hand side of Lake Bennett should be followed until Cariboo Crossing is reached. Here there is a stream connecting Lake Bennett with Lake Tagish, and near by is a well worn trail used by bands of Cariboo in their annual or biennial excursions. The connecting river is about two miles long, and quite sluggish. In Lake Tagish we keep near the left hand shore for about eighteen miles, and then enter a river which is about six miles long. About half way is Tagish House, a large Indian council house, several huts

LAKE BENNETT

A panorama of the community looking north, showing Abbott's Cove.

and a burial ground, usually deserted, but belonging to the Stick tribe of Indians. The river is wide and sluggish, and in some places quite shallow. We emerge into Lake Marsh or Mud Lake, through which we follow the left bank twenty-five miles to the head of a wide river, the Lewis. On Marsh Lake, if it be summer, we learn most completely the suction capacity of the famed Yukon mosquito. But now we are through it and well on our way down the Lewis we have something else to think of, for about twenty miles of the river having been passed we are approaching the worst danger points of the whole journey.

Miles Cañon and White Horse Rapids

About twenty five miles, or a little less, below Lake Marsh, a wall of mountains rises up, and the river, which has been about two hundred yards in width, is suddenly confined within a space of less than fifty feet. This is the famous and deservedly dreaded Miles Cañon, in which scores have been drowned. It is three quarters of a mile long, and about half way down there is a sudden widening of the channel into short curved bays on each side, then a contraction of the cañon to its original narrowness until it emerges into the broad river. At the enlarged centre the rushing waters spread out and have a terrific suction toward the sides, and then when the canon narrows again the waters plunge into the confined outlet with seething violence. Some go through the cañon safely, some attempt it and die, and others take the only safe course and make a portage. As we approach the cañon we *keep to the right*. If we decide to "shoot" the cañon we lighten our boat of part of its load, use our efforts to keep in the middle of the channel, and in about two minutes the boat and its occupants will be through the cañon or else sucked down in that powerful current. My advice is — don't!

MILES CANYON, LEWES RIVER (YUKON RIVER)

On the right hand side, about one hundred feet above the cañon, there is a smooth trail along a bench, which many hundreds of Yukoners have used in making a portage. If we follow their example, three or four hours will suffice to get boat and outfit over the trail, with everything safe and sound. It is a little work, but none of the party is missing.

Keep to the left

Our troubles, however, are not yet over, for having emerged from Miles Cañon it is only between two and three miles to the White Horse Rapids. *Keep to the left!* As soon as we reach smooth water on the left bank we tie up and look for a place to make a portage.

Some run the rapids; but many of those who have attempted it have drowned. The portage is not long and the danger to be avoided is equal to that just passed through at Miles Cañon. Near the rapids there is a plane of rock, near the river, which is often used to line the boats through the rapids. This will do at a very low stage of water, but even then is dangerous. If the water is high, disaster is more than likely and many a boat has been dashed to pieces on the rocks or swamped in the waters when its owner has tried to line it down.

The best way is to make a portage of a hundred yards or so to safe water, and a little below is another stretch of equal danger around which a portage should also be made. It is about half a mile through White Horse Rapids.

On to the Yukon

The worst dangers of the journey are now over and the boat glides on, with a swift current, sixteen miles to the confluence of the Tahkeena River and then twelve miles further until we reach Lake La Barge.

MILES CANYON, YUKON RIVER (FORMERLY, LEWES RIVER)

WHITEHORSE RAPIDS, YUKON RIVER

It will be understood that we have been talking about the summer trip. Those who come in during March or April, before the thaw beings, will make the journey from Chilkoot Pass as far as Lake La Barge, if possible with sleds. They will then stop here, with the worst dangers of the journey past, to build their boat for the down river trip.

Lake La Barge is a very beautiful sheet of water, thirty miles in length and from five to ten miles in width. At its end we emerge into the river again, and after a run of thirty miles come to the junction of the Hootalinqua River. There are numerous rocks in this thirty miles, but after that it is plain sailing until at 135 miles below we reach the Five Fingers Rapids. For five miles before reaching them a marked acceleration of the current is noticeable. Keep close to the right bank and make a landing. If the load is heavy it should be lightened before attempting to go through.

Danger ahead

Five Fingers is an obstruction caused by a ledge of rock lying directly across the stream with five openings in it. There are four rocks of large size standing in a row across the river. If not too heavily loaded these rapids can be passed without any difficulty. *Keep to the right.*

Three miles below are the Rink Rapids. *Keep to the right*. There is no danger here, nor is there any more to the end of our journey. Below Rink Rapids we have the smoothest kind of travelling all the way to the mouth of the Klondike, which is about two hundred and thirty miles. We go on the first fifty-five miles, and the Pelly River coming in and joining the Lewis, we are on the main Yukon. The other important streams are the White, Stewart, Sixty-Mile and Indian Rivers, all streams of golden repute and then — The Klondike and Dawson City.

Chapter X

Dawson City

Description of the metropolis of the Yukon

When you get to Dawson City you are in a typical mining camp, with all that the name implies. Of course there are differences in mining camps, but they are for the greater part climatic, and the general characteristics of mining camps have always been about the same — from Hangtown to Dawson.

Some differences will be noted at Dawson which are due to surrounding circumstances. One of the most noteworthy is the absence of "shooting scrapes." In the boom times of Hangtown, Washoe, Tombstone, Deadwood, Leadville and Creede they had, as the saying went, "a man for breakfast every morning." This prevalence of lawlessness in the mining camps in the United States is largely an evil arising from the too literal carrying out of democratic principles. Those who are at work in the mines are too busy to attend to matters of law and order, and as a consequence, the new settlement is largely run, in its earlier days, by the lawless elements in the community, the "sure-thing" gambler, the cappers and loafers, and the professional "desperado", who puts in his intervals between stage robbing and claim jumping and loafing around saloons, and who poses as a bad man "from Bitter Creek" until in some quarrel, he is killed.

Only one serious affray

The Klondike discoveries were made in September, and from that time until the boats came out in June only one serious affray occurred. A man was shot in the back by a vicious character, who was immediately arrested by the Canadian Mounted Police, and was awaiting trial for

DAWSON CITY

felonious assault, at last account, his victim having recovered.

There are many and just complaints about the hard rules enforced by Canada in respect to mining claims on the Yukon, but on the other hand, the protection afforded by their agencies of law and order cannot be too highly commended.

Dawson is laid out in rectangular shape into lots and 66 foot streets, and has been regularly entered as a town site by Joseph Ladue, its proprietor, and town-lots are as good as gold, for they bring, in favourable locations, as high as $5,000 apiece. It lies on low ground on the east bank of the Yukon, a short distance below the mouth of the Klondike River. The principal part of the inhabitants live in tents, temporarily, although a good many houses have gone up, many of them being finer than anything heretofore known on the Yukon. Yet the best of them would be considered poor affairs in almost any civilized

ONE OF THE FIRST HOUSES IN DAWSON CITY

towns or villages in the United States. The most pretentious of them are the saloons, except the large warehouses built by the two trading companies.

The latter do a big business. They control the means of ingress for all kinds of merchandise, and while they have been straining every resource to get provisions through to meet the big influx of people who are coming in from every direction, while they have practically a monopoly on the business, they do not use it oppressively, although when a shortage comes they put up prices to steep figures until it is relieved.

"Four bits" the minimum coin

The lowest measure of value in actual use at Dawson is "four bits" or fifty cents. It is the price of the smallest articles. They say that a newcomer who had arrived via the river and whose nether garments were out of repair went to one of the stores and called for a needle, which he got, and then asked what was the price.

"Four bits", was the sterotyped response.

"Isn't that pretty steep?" asked the tenderfoot.

The freight that counts

"Well, you see, my friend," said the storekeeper, "it ain't the first cost of the needle that counts, but it's the freight."

Prices of commodities fluctuate at Dawson, as elsewhere, in accordance with the inexorable law of supply and demand, except whisky, which is stable at "four bits" a drink, and you can fill the glass to the rim if you want to. The demand never fails nor the supply. If the latter should threaten a shortage, the river is near by and strength would be allowed to suffer rather than quantity.

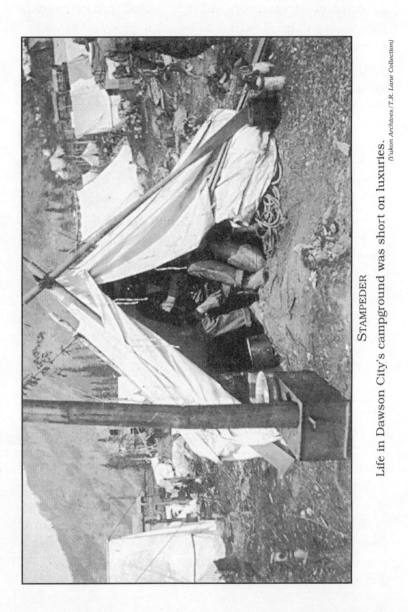

(Yukon Archives / T.R. Lane Collection)

STAMPEDER

Life in Dawson City's campground was short on luxuries.

Scale of prices

As to other commodities, they are all proportionately high. Joseph Ladue, who has been merchandising on the Yukon for years, has prepared the following scale of prices:[1]

Flour, per 100 lbs.	$12.00
Moose hams, per pound	1.00
Caribou meat, per pound	.65
Beans, per pound	.10
Rice, per pound	.25
Sugar, per pound	.25
Bacon, per pound	.40
Butter, per roll	1.50
Eggs, per dozen	1.50
Better eggs, per dozen	2.00
Salmon, each	$1 to 1.50
Potatoes, per pound	.25
Turnips, per pound	.15
Tea, per pound	1.00
Coffee, per pound	.50
Dried fruits, per pound	.35
Canned fruits	.50
Canned meats	.75
Lemons, each	.20
Oranges, each	.50
Tobacco, per pound	1.50
Liquors, per drink	.50
Shovels	2.50
Picks	5.00
Coal oil, per gallon	1.00
Overalls	1.50
Underwear, per suit	$5 to 7.50
Shoes	5.00
Rubber boots	$10 to 15.00

Along in the late spring, when the supply runs down to a low ebb, these prices may be doubled or more.

---

(1) If one were to multiply these prices by a factor of 25 to compare them to today's prices, it would become clearer just what the cost of living was. For instance, flour would work out to be $3.00 per pound; oranges, $12.50; butter, $37.50; and rubber boots at least $250.00.

Lumber at last quotations was worth $150 per thousand feet, rough; $250 planed. Wages in town $10 per day for unskilled labour, $15 for carpenters and $15 for work in the mines; but it was thought wages would get lower with the big arrivals of new people. Logs are worth $30 per thousand feet, log measure at the mill. The sawmill at Dawson is of small capacity, and although it is kept running day and night it is away behind its orders.

BRINGING HOME THEIR GOLD

Much carousing going on

Dawson is what is called "a lively camp". Liveliness, in this connection, largely means drunkenness and carousing. Those who have lived in "flush" mining camps will be able to picture the scene for themselves. The people coming to town are of heterogeneous assortment. The first man you meet, rough in garb and grizzled in appearance, may be a graduate of a good college, a scion of a first class family, and a man who can interestingly discuss subjects of literature, science and culture. The next, arrayed in the "boiled shirt" only recently introduced into the Yukon, and costing a dollar to launder, is probably the "barkeep" of a favourite saloon, or the "piano thumper" of the biggest dance house.

The saloons are of mining camp type. In front the bar, with a pair of gold scales at the end. Back of that the dance is going on, and either a piano that has seen better days, or a violin that would better have never occurred at all, is constantly going. "Git your pardners for a cowtillion", yells a loud voice, which follows with "Balance all! Alaman left! Ladies chain!" and so on, concluding with "Promenade all — to the bar!"

They make the numbers short and lively, so as to make the last call come as frequently as possible.

In the back part of the room are the gambling layouts, the poker games and the other devices by which the miners are inveigled to give up all or a large share of their dust to the boiled shirt gentry who toil not.

Not all miners are patrons of these establishments. Quite a large share of those who are now delving in the mines of the district are men of industry and purpose who came in with a "grub stake" and are straining every nerve for a "home stake," looking perhaps to the relieving of a family pinched by poverty, a mother in humble circumstances, or a loyal sweetheart who waits and watches; all thinking of some one on "the outside." It is queer that home should be so designated. In Arizona, before the era of railroads, when the only means of communication was by buckboard over the desert to the end of the railroad at Los Angeles, we used to call the trip to San Francisco "going inside." Up on the Yukon they recognised the completeness of their isolation by saying that one coming to the States is "going outside".

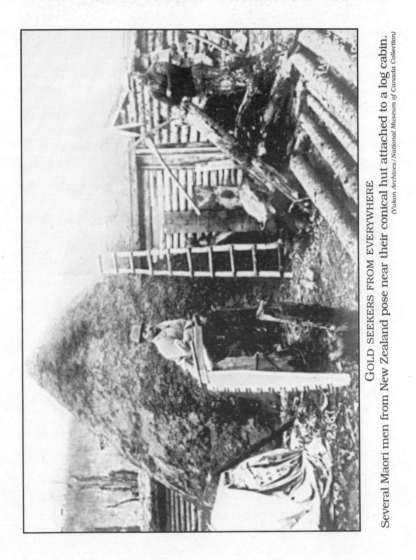

GOLD SEEKERS FROM EVERYWHERE

Several Maori men from New Zealand pose near their conical hut attached to a log cabin.

(Yukon Archives / National Museum of Canada Collection)

THE CARMACK FAMILY
George, Kate and daughter, Graphie.
(Yukon Archives/A.C. Johnson Collection)

The Discoverer of Bonanza

In Dawson, as in other mining towns, there is the loafer who has no mine, no home, nothing but a consuming thirst, which he is waiting for some other person to gratify. To him, as a boon, comes the miner, usually an old timer, who has something besides room in his dust sack and who is willing to set 'em up. The latter goes from saloon to saloon with quite a retinue. One of the most generous of these "producers" is said to be

George McCormack, owner of the Discovery on Bonanza Creek. He is a man of some intelligence and an old timer on the river, with an Indian wife and several brown faced youngsters. He used to have a little store on the river above "Five Finger Rapids," where he traded with the Indians, and he did some work in developing a coal vein in the same neighbourhood. He was engaged at the Indian village at the mouth of the Klondike in drying salmon for a living prior to making the great strike on Bonanza. The old timers call him "Stick George," because of his close relationship with the Stick Indians; but just now he is being made much of by the "rounders" of the camp, and in frontier fashion George frequently "treats the crowd" at an expense sometimes as much as $50 per treat. Even a discovery claim on the Bonanza will not stand that long.

There are men of all sorts and conditions in Dawson, and of all shades of opinion. Many are old Pacific coast miners, and therefore ardent believers in free coinage theories. Many of them think that the gold of the Yukon region is so plentiful that it will cause gold to be demonetised. Some of those who came out with a "home stake" last summer made the trip with a view to getting the value of their money while it was good.

Women in the camp

There are several good women at Dawson and the mines near by — most of them with their husbands, whose fortunes they are sharing, but a few of them working in various useful ways to improve their own fortunes.

The women who have been brave enough to go to the frozen north with their husbands are of the kind to prove valuable aids to them, and some of the most fortunate men in the gulches are included among the married men.

The Canadian law does not recognise a married woman's property rights, and she cannot locate a claim in addition to her husband's, but the aid which she extends in giving the home atmosphere even to a lonely hut on the confines of the Arctic Circle is as good as a gold mine.

The good luck of the married miners has made a deep impression upon the bachelor ones. Some have left sweethearts at home, many others are heart-whole and fancy-free, but very impressionable. An unmarried woman of good character who goes to the Yukon will have to stand a constant siege of admirers. I do not say this in order to start a stampede of spinsters to the new El Dorado, but merely as a veracious recorder of the facts surrounding the social life at Dawson City.

Bridget struck it rich

I give the following story at second-hand, but it is too good not to be true.

"P.B. Weare, of Chicago, head of the North American Transportation and Trading Company, says some women do well in the Klondike region. A year ago he and Mrs. Weare rejoice in the possession of a cook, whose name was Bridget. One day Bridget announced her intention of going to Alaska. Mr. Weare remonstrated. 'You can't mine,' he said.

" 'That's true,' answered the woman, 'but there's them that can.'

"A woman of stylish appearance and haughty demeanour swished her silken skirts past the admiring office boy in Mr. Weare's office last Thursday, and extended a primrose-gloved hand to the stout man who sat at the desk. Looking up, he recognised his old cook.

"She told him that before she had got fifty miles up the Yukon she had received 125 proposals of marriage, and that she had held off until an engaging compatriot, with a Kerry brogue and a mine that panned at the rate of $50,000 a month, swore that he could not live without her. 'I am now on my way to Europe,' said Bridget, 'and I thought I'd like to see you as I went through. You mind what I told you when I left?'

In a mining camp, however rough, women of good repute are accorded the highest deference.

The disreputable element

In Dawson, however, all the women are not of the class named, and the "dance hall fairies" are among the most demoralizing elements of the town. These characters follow successful gold mining everywhere. Inspector Constantine, head of the Mounted Police, succeeds in keeping the disreputable element within bounds. The women who went into Dawson wore bloomers over the mountain, and when they reached the city they made up their minds to adopt the costume altogether, thus appearing in the streets and dance halls. But Captain Constantine gave orders that either bloomers or their wearers must go, and the women took to abbreviated skirts instead.

The currency is gold dust. The stores and saloons have gold-scales at the end of counter and bar. The saloons issue chips which are good at the bar or in the gambling game. The miner brings in his sack and leaves it behind the bar, saying, "Give me five hundred," or whatever amount he thinks he requires. When he wants his gold again he returns the unused chips and pays for what he owes.

The summer at Dawson is a queer season, because the sun never sets and one can read a newspaper without artificial light at every hour of the twenty-four.

PROSTITUTES
Many women came to the Klondike to cash in
on the fortunes of the miners.
(British Columbia Archives / Larss and Duclos Collection)

DEAD HORSE, DAWSON CITY
Nine men work with ropes to remove a dead horse from the mud.

The famous Yukon mosquito is a terror for some time after the snow melts, but becomes less troublesome in the latter part of the summer. When in full training he is a ferocious demon in comparison with whom the famous Jersey variety is a cooing innocent.

Before the snow melted last spring an enterprising cattleman from Juneau drove in a herd of forty beeves from the coast and slaughtered them. The beef went readily at from 50 to 75 cents a pound.

New finds bring stampedes

The daily excitement in Klondike, outside of that around the saloons, consists of the news that comes in from the various gulches and creeks. A man will bring news of promising discoveries of "pay gravel" anywhere from ten to fifty miles or more away. Then begins a stampede; picks, shovels, pans and several days' provisions are packed up and a hundred men are on their way to the creek or gulch where the "find" is supposed to be. Some of these trips end in disgust, but so many have turned out well that the camp is kept in a continual state of excitement. Dominion Creek, a branch of Indian River, and Henderson Creek emptying into the Yukon near the mouth of Stewart River, called out quite a host of gold hunters and are said to prospect well.

Too-Much-Gold Creek

One of the most common subjects of discussion during the early summer was as to the location of Too- Much-Gold Creek. The name came from an Indian yarn that in "Bonanza much gold, in Hunker Creek more gold, and in long creek, higher up, too much gold" — "too much" being an Indian superlative.

Along in the latter part of June a creek emptying into the Klondike about thirty five miles up was explored and many claims located toward its head waters. It is said to prospect well. They named it Too-Much-Gold Creek.

These continual finds keep Dawson agog. It is noticeable that "tenderfoot" is no longer a title of disrespect in the camp. So many utter "greenhorns" have made strikes that some of the old timers are disgusted. The experienced miners thought Bonanza Creek was too wide to be much account, but their theories have been entirely upset by the results. "I'll tell you what, boys," said one of them, "you can't tell anything about gold. You're just as likely to find it where it ain't as where it is!"

Shut out from civilization

Dawson is very anxious to hear from the outside world. Steamers are few and far between and newspapers are a luxury. The mail comes to Circle City, and it costs a dollar a letter to get the mail in and out. The Dominion government, however, has ordered the establishing of a post office, and mail matters will be much aided and expedited.

When books and papers arrive in camp, they are read and reread and handed about until they are worn out. Those who wearily pack goods over mountains and down rapids, are for the most part meagerly supplied in the way of libraries.

When the long, dark winter comes on, Dawson will have a larger resident population, but less visitors. If the food supply keeps up the town will be gay. Its rowdy features will perhaps become more pronounced, but the police force is to be augmented, and Captain Constantine, while pursuing a liberal policy, keeps a rigid control over any tendency toward more serious disorder.

The most noteworthy feature of the camp is the rigid honesty and trustfulness that have so far prevailed. Gold sacks representing thousands of dollars in value are thrown

WINTER ROUTE TO THE MINES WITH DOG SLEDS

REINDEER HERD REACHES DAWSON CITY

In 1897, a group of Laplanders reach Dawson City with a herd of reindeer.

under counters and bars without being weighed or counted, and yet these deposits have been as safe and sacred as if they had been placed in safety vaults of the most modern build.

Dawson is a rough place in a rough country, but it holds a very large number of men of the best and noblest type, with the physical endowments and character to achieve great and brave things.

Horses, dogs and reindeer

One of the things which will especially impress the newcomer is the absence of horses. There have been horses in the Yukon valley, but they do not do well. The severe winters crack their hoofs so that they are useless, and horses driven in during the summer are usually killed for dog meat in the winter, bringing about fifteen cents a pound.

There are dogs. You find them of every kind and degree, but they are highly valued because they are about the only beasts of burden in that section. Rev. Sheldon Jackson, who has been in Alaska for years in charge of Indian educational affairs on behalf of the government, has been bringing reindeer from Siberia for domestication as a government enterprise, but the project has not yet sufficiently advanced to make reindeer a factor in the transportation facilities of the country. Some will be sent to Circle City next winter, but Dawson City being in Canada, none will go there.

No firearms

Another very noticeable feature, which is a leading one in the prevention of crime and disorder, is the absence of firearms. In the old-time Pacific Coast mining towns the six-shooter was regarded as indispensable. But in Dawson the rule against firearms is rigidly enforced by the Mounted Police. There is no necessity for a pistol either in town or outside of it. The natives are all peaceable, and the game is better hunted with rifle and shotgun. The absence of pistols is the very best feature of the management of affairs at Dawson.

The region around Dawson is very well timbered. The trees are not large, and the logs for the mill come from points higher up the river, but the supply for fuel comes from points near by. The high cost of labor in cutting and hauling, however, brings the price of fuel up to $25 per cord in Dawson.

Social features of Dawson

The religious element is not predominant in Dawson City, by any means, but it is not entirely absent. Missions have been established by the Church of England (Episcopal) and the Roman Catholics, and regular services are held.

New business enterprises are being established almost every day, the saloons being the most numerous. Two or three of the larger ones have most of the trade, and Harry Ash, who moved his dancing establishment and saloon from Circle City to Dawson, is said to be taking in from $2,000 to $3,000 per day. There is no midnight closing ordinance in Dawson and the wet goods establishments keep continually open.

The store of the Alaska Commercial Company carries a large stock of goods and is in charge of Captain J.E. Hansen, an energetic young business man who understands the wants of the country.

Capital John J. Healy

The business of the North American Transportation and Trading Company at Dawson is in personal charge of Captain John J. Healy. He was the originator of the company and enlisted the aid of Portus B. Weare and John Cudahy, Chicago capitalists, in its organization. Out on the Yukon the formal title is seldom used. They call it "Captain Healy's Company."

Captain Healy has led a life of adventure. He was born in Ireland fifty five years ago, but was brought to the United States by his parents when a very small boy. The spirit of adventure was innate in him, and when twelve years of age he ran away from home to join Walker's famous band of filibusters, bound for Nicaragua. Later he went to Salt Lake City with Johnson's army to assist in disciplining the Mormons. From that time he was a foremost figure among the pioneers of the "untrodden west." He discovered the Salmon River gold fields in Idaho and was first at the Last Chance leads in Montana. From the later place he prospected up the Saskatchewan. There he saw a tempting opportunity to trade with the Blackfeet Indians. He established Fort Whoopup and became so popular with the Indians that for many years the powerful Hudson Bay Company did not venture to invade his territory, although eager to drive him from the field of competition. Later he became sheriff of Choteau County, Montana, in the wildest days of that region. He became a terror to outlaws, and it is said of him that no bandit was ever "quick enough to get the drop on Johnny Healy."

There are few sections of the west which he has not traversed as a miner, trapper or trader, and where he is not known.

From Montana Captain Healy went to Alaska and established, at the head of Chilkoot Inlet, south of the pass of the same name, a store still known as "Healy's Store," at what is now called Dyea. He was up on the Yukon years ago and became impressed with its richness as a gold bearing region; and since the establishing of the North American Trading and Transportation Company has been a leader in the development of the country.

Mrs. Healy and her mine

Captain Healy has a wife and an established home at Dawson, having moved there from Fort Cudahy. It is noteworthy that he was really the first to try mining in the vicinity of Dawson. Opposite the mouth of the Klondike he located, about five years ago, a quartz ledge, which carries copper and some gold. Out on the Yukon the appetite for quartz mines has even yet not been fully developed, and Captain Healy let the time expire without doing his "assessment work" within the time prescribed by law. It was safe enough, however for Yukoners had not acquired the claim-jumping habit. About a year after locating his claim Captain Healy and his wife were making a trip on the steamer to Sixty-Mile and he told Mrs. Healy about the claim, but said that he had not worked it and did not think he would, as it was "too early to bother with quartz."

Mrs. Healy told her husband that if he did not want the mine she did, and she relocated it, named it the "Four Leaf Clover Mine", and became the possessor of a ledge eight feet wide from wall to wall, with all its "dips, spurs and angles," turning out rock rich in copper and carrying from $10 to $15 a ton in gold, as far as prospected. The development has been done by tunnelling, and the mine is locally known as "Captain Healy's tunnel."

Other enterprises at Dawson

Besides the general stores and saloons there are other business enterprises. The one blacksmith shop is doing a rushing business, as active mining calls for a considerable amount of work of that kind. A barber shop, bakery and laundry also flourish.

It used to be the proud claim of mining camps of '49 on the Sierras that they were so healthful that it was necessary to "kill a man to start a graveyard," without which no city could be considered full fledged. Dawson however, has a cemetery already established. William Stickney and partner started from Juneau to go up the Yukon last winter and Stickney died from exposure on Lake La Barge. His partner tried to get aid to take the body up to Dawson, but failed, and made the trip alone. Stickney's body was the first buried in Dawson.

Health of Dawson City

In spite of the rigor of the climate, Dawson may be considered a very healthy city. The winter is severe and uncomfortable, but to those who are warmly clad and well housed, and who are careful of themselves, the cold season is the one when there is least sickness. Scurvy, resulting from the lack of fresh meat and vegetables, is the complaint most prevalent, both on the road and in the mining camps. It can be easily prevented, however, by the use of lime juice (which costs $2.50 quart bottle in Dawson), or still better, by using citric acid flavoured with lemon, making pleasant lemonade which is, at the same time, the best antiscorbutic medicine known. Those who go to Dawson should procure at least a pound of citric acid crystals and two ounces of oil of lemons.

Some get rheumatism from exposure, although that disease is not greatly prevalent, and there is no malaria. Early in the summer there is some biliousness and constipation, but the amount of sickness is not great, although a resident physician who went to Dawson from Circle City and Police Surgeon A.E. Wills both have a good practice. They carry their own supplies of staple drugs and medicines and compound their own prescriptions. Common remedies and patent medicines are carried at the trading stores.

Surgeon Wills, in a report to the Canadian government, says of the health of the country:

"The diseases most met with in this country are
dyspepsia, anaemia; scurvy caused by improperly cooked
food, sameness of diet, overwork, want of fresh vegetables,
overheated and badly ventilated houses; rheumatism,
pneumonia, bronchitis, and teritis, cystitis, and other
acute diseases, from exposure to wet and cold; debility
and chronic diseases, due to excesses. One case of
typhoid fever occurred in Forty-Mile last fall, probably due
to drinking water polluted with decayed vegetable matter."

New features of the town

During the winter there was a lodging house in
Dawson, occupying a long, low building of logs. It is being
replaced by a larger and more comfortable structure.
There are two or three restaurants in Dawson. The staple
charge for a meal is $1.50 unless the customer wants
luxuries, then the bill is proportionately increased.

One of the greatest needs of the town is proper
facilities for sending money to the States, but this will
likely not last longer than next spring, when Wells, Fargo
& Co. will establish a branch in Dawson and furnish the
opportunity for miners to send money home safely.

A newspaper is one of the things that will be started if
the adventurous thought-moulders who are dragging
Washington hand-presses over the pass get through.

Chapter XI

How Women Fare

Experiences of Mrs. Berry and Mrs. Gage
told by themselves

Her novel experience of going over the divide and living in a mining camp in the frozen north as a wedding trip makes anything from Mrs. Berry, "the bride of the Klondike," especially interesting, and as many women have expressed a desire to go to the "land of the midnight sun" in search of fame and fortune, they will like to hear her experiences in her own words. She was asked to give her opinion upon the subject of the proposed feminine exodus to the north.

Advice to women

"What advice would I give to a woman about going to Alaska?" she said pleasantly. "Why, to stay away, of course. It's no place for a woman. I mean for a woman alone; one who goes to make a living or a fortune. Yes, there are women going into the mines alone, there were when we came out, all with the hope of getting big pay. It's much better for a man, though, if he has a wife along. Whatever stories of miserable living and excessive hardships there are, are about the poor fellows who had not sufficient outfit or suffered by their own poor cooking.

"The men are not much at cooking up there, and, that is the reason they suffer with stomach troubles, and, as some say they did, with scurvy. After a man has worked hard all day in the diggings he doesn't feel much like cooking a nice meal when he goes to his cabin, cold, tired and hungry, and finds no fire in the stove and all the food frozen.

Clothes suited for the trip

"I took an outfit of clothes made especially for the trip. I got everything of the best material, and found it paid in the long run. One doesn't need a great deal, and it is best to take no more than is actually necessary on account of the trouble and expense of carrying the things. My outfit cost about $250. It included three suits of everything, right straight through.

"I had very heavy woollen underwear and knitted woollen stockings. My skirts were made short, only a little below the knee. I had a heavy fur coat of marten, a fur cape, fur gloves and the heaviest shawl I could get. Shoes are not necessary, except to go to Juneau and come back from there. My fur coat I took from here, because, strange as it may seem, furs cost less and are better here than in Alaska.

"A fur robe is necessary. We got one up there from a man coming out, but it is just as well for any one going up to take one along. The fur gloves can be had up there better than here, however, and cost about $3. Moccasins are worn instead of shoes through the winter and muclues when it is thawing and wet. They are both to be had there at from $1 to $4 or $5 a pair. The moccasins are made of fur seal, 'with the furry side inside and the inside out,' like Minnehaha's clothing. They come to the knee, or half way or all the way up the thigh, as you choose. They are slipped on like a boot, and from the instep the thongs go across round the leg, like the old fashioned sandals, and tie at the top, where there is also a draw string.

"The muclues — that's the native name for them — are the mud moccasins. The soles are made waterproof with seal oil. If a woman keeps her feet warm her health is pretty safe, and for that reason, in addition to the woollen

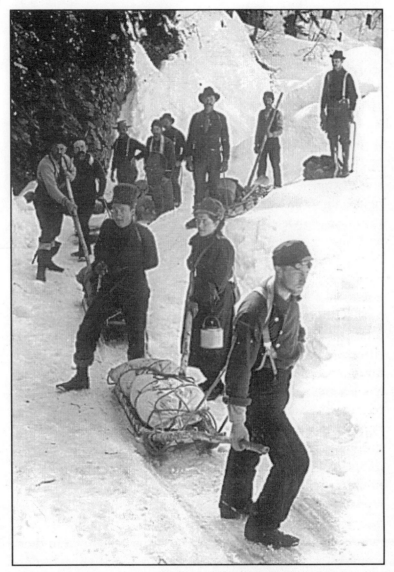

CHILKOOT CLIMB
Men and women worked side by side at the tough work. Belinda Mulroney
(forefront) became the most successful business person in the Klondike.

(Yukon Archives / Winter and Pond Collection)

stockings and moccasins, I wore also flannel insoles. In all the time I was in Alaska I never suffered from frostbite — didn't even get my fingers nipped or my nose — and I wore no veil all the time I was there. I took a good medicine chest with me, too."

Three months with dog team

"We left Juneau last March with several friends, our supplies and a dog team. I put on my Alaska uniform there, the heavy flannels, warm dress with short skirt, moccasins, fur coat, cap and gloves, kept my shawl handy to roll up in case it storms, and was rolled in a full robe and bound to the sled, so when it rolled over I rolled with it, and many tumbles in the snow I got that way. The supplies for Mr. Berry and myself included his clothes, my small furs, our stove and all our food, cost about $800 and weighed about 2,000 pounds. We did not confine ourselves to a bean-and-bacon diet. We had plenty of canned meats, hams, bacon, dried fruits, and vegetables and all sorts of canned things besides. We arranged for as wholesome a diet as possible with canned goods.

"It took us three months of travel from Juneau to Forty-Mile, a distance of about nine hundred miles, I think. We travelled ten or twelve and occasionally fifteen miles a day. We couldn't do more because the dogs wouldn't stand it. Up to the summit we carried our own stores, and on the other side hired Indians. We had fresh meat on the way — moose and caribou.

"At first when I saw the dirty natives bringing it in their canoes I could not bring myself to eat it, but I soon changed my mind and got to like it. We prepared our meals by setting up our stove right on the ice, in the open sometimes, and at others pitched a tent and did our cooking under cover, then up stakes and on again. At night we pitched our tents, made a bed of boughs, put blankets on, rolled ourselves in blankets, covered ourselves with the fur robes and slept well. We had four pairs of heavy blankets, and I took two small pillows along.

"Our bedding was always packed in an oil skin cover, and so kept dry all the way. The best time made was across La Barge Lake. We crossed the thirty-six miles in a night. They put the tent upon the provision scow for me, and I went to bed in it and slept all the way across the Lewis River. We had to make such good time because we were afraid the ice would begin to run and the boats go under.

"We had a fine sunshiny day to cross the summit, but we had to sit still and wait two weeks for it. We got to Forty-Mile in June and went to the Klondike in October. I stayed at the post, now Dawson City, while the boys went on to build a cabin. It took us two days to walk the nineteen miles to the diggings. There was about an inch of water on the ice and I slipped and slid in every direction going over."

Housekeeping on the Klondike

"When I got there the house had no door, windows or floor, and I had to stand around outside until a hole was cut for me to get in through. We had a two room house, and after it was fixed up it was very comfortable for Klondike. The boys had a carpet and curtain sent over for me. We had all the camp-made furniture we needed, a bed and stove — a long, little sheet iron affair, with two holes on top and a drum to bake in. The wood is so full of pitch — it's the meanest, knottiest, scrubbiest wood I ever saw — that the fire burns up and goes out if you turn your back on it for a minute. The water we used was all snow or ice, and had to be thawed. If any one wanted a drink, a chunk of ice had to be thawed and cooled again.

"The stores that were kept in the cache to save them

BONANZA
George Carmack blazed this small spruce tree in front
of his family's crude cabin, and wrote on it in pencil:
"TO WHOM IT MAY CONCERN
"I do, this day, locate and claim, by right of discovery,
five hundred feet, running upstream from this notice,
located this 17th day of August, 1896."

(Yukon Archives/A.C. Johnson Collection)

from the wild animals were frozen, of course, and had to be thawed out before being cooked. The things we wanted to keep from freezing we had to keep warm in the house. Some wines and a case of champagne were sent us for Christmas and I had to keep them under my bed to save them from freezing.

"The canned and dried things were very tiresome eating. We had fresh meat now and then and some beef, for last winter was the first time that beef was sent across the pass. We had a nice roast for our New Year dinner and fruit cake, mince pie and nuts and raisins, as well as the usual canned vegetables.

"The men had hard times making bread, and I taught several of them how to make yeast bread. We could get hops and canned potatoes, and it was easy enough to make yeast, but how I did long for a raw potato — anything fresh and green. We didn't lack for visitors at the mines. I had nine to luncheon with me there before I even had a table to eat off, and one time it was so that strangers would come and eat — even come and take any food in sight, and bolt with it. We had some one staying at our house nearly every night, for people were always passing through, and they had to have shelter."

How to Bathe at the Klondike

"The cabins didn't have all the modern improvements by any means; no porcelain tubs or hot or cold water. When we wanted a bath we melted ice, heated the water, got the pan in that we used for washing the gold and did our bathing in that. I was not sick once during all the time I was there, except slight indispositions, and I'm twenty five pounds heavier now than when I went up, and feel better than ever.

"I went out nearly every day when I had finished my housework. I would hunt the dumps for nuggets, or else pan gold. I'd have to melt the water for that, and at first I lost half the gold, but after a time I learned to get it all out. Things were very high part of the winter. At one time we paid $60 for a fifty pound sack of flour, and 23 cents a pound extra for portage, and were glad to get it. I paid $6 a yard for dress goods and $300 for having a skirt made. Oh, yes, there are dressmakers even up there. They sew for the natives — make the siwash red and blue satin dresses for them, all in the same style, a tight basque, buttoned straight down the front, and a skirt.

"Eight months of the year it is dark up there, with only about four hours light each day. There is a gray twilight and the men work through that, but we often had to light the lamps at half-past 1 or 2 in the afternoon. We had oil lamps, but the majority use candles.

Winter is healthy

"In the winter the Yukon is one of the healthiest places for any one going there with sound health, but when the summer comes it is unhealthy. It is damp, the water is bad, it gets very hot, and the mosquitoes are awful.

"Coming away from the mines we made the distance between them and Dawson in one night, but the trail is so bad that, notwithstanding I wore a skirt only knee length, I was covered with mud to the waist. Dawson may have been a quiet city once, but when I came through it was in such a rowdy state that it was impossible for me to go to my meals and I had to have them sent to me. Men and women — there were about fifty women there — were carousing continually. The people who follow on the heels of the good, steady-going, hard-working miners are among the worst up there.

"There are good women too, many who have gone with their husbands. On the Bonanza, near us, there is still a lovely, beautiful woman — Mrs. Galvin, of Helena, Mont. and I was sorry to leave her when I came away.

"Would I go to the Yukon again? Never. I am glad I had the experience I really did. It was worth the roughing, but once is enough. I'll stay with my mother in Fresno when Mr. Berry goes back in the spring. He will only go from spring to fall after this. I'll stay down here and spend the money when he brings it out."

MRS. E.F. GAGE

Another brave woman

Mrs. Eli Gage, wife of the son of Lyman J. Gage, Secretary of the United States Treasury, was in the Klondike region when the great finds were made and knows all about the excitement, the stirring scenes and wonderful developments of the winter of 1896 in that far off northern country.

Her husband is auditor of the North American Transportation and Trading Company and his duties are in Alaska. His wife will return in the spring in company with Clarence J. Berry and Frank Phiscator, two of the most fortunate of the Klondike bonanza kings, with whom she returned on the treasure ship "Portland" in July. Her views in regard to the country and the doings of its people will be found of great interest.

She likes frontier life

"It is wonderful how fascinating the life on the frontier becomes," she said the other morning. "The man or woman who gets a taste of it and succeeds and thrives by it rarely gets to like anything else. It may be a barbarous confession, but it seems to me that the kindest, most considerate and most practically honest people that I ever met are the miners who are risking all at one throw in the work on the Klondike. It was here that I saw a code of honor which made all men honest — a life in which each man must live a fair part or get a forcible and roughly polite invitation to move.

"It takes men of sturdy character to get into the valley, and the virtues which they cling to are ones from which they want no man to part. I do not think that I heard of a single case in my summer's stay in upper Alaska where prospectors and diggers had been guilty of dishonesty. It may be that honesty is a trait which thrives because it is backed by the point of a gun, but it is there nevertheless. Explorers going to the field or miners coming out frequently undertake greater loads than the teams can pull through. It is the custom at such times to put the surplus at the roadside and go on with half. The part left behind is perfectly safe until it shall be called for. I doubt that this rule would work in Chicago or other civilised places.

Treasure brought back

"Mr. Phiscator and Mr. Berry were on the *Portland* — the ship which brought the $1,000,000 cargo of yellow metal into Seattle. It is not likely that one man in fifty could picture these two men as they are. The usual thing would be to have them half — savage, uncouth and hardened by a long season away from men and the world. This sort of description would not fit either in the slightest particular. They are both modest, decidedly bashful and lack all the traits which the tenderfoot gives to the real miner. They have no boastings to make — and this in face of the fact that it is more than likely the next year will prove they are among the richest men in this country.

"It is probable that they were the money kings of the Portland, although the ship's safe and the captain's stateroom were filled to overflowing with the earnings of other members of the passenger crew. It was like an actual representation of the air castles of fairyland. There was gold stacked upon gold, nuggets and in dust, tied up in old sacks and held in bottles with the corks sealed. I asked the captain if he did not fear to carry such a load of pure money. He said he feared nothing so long as he knew he had no one aboard but miners.

From poverty to affluence

"It was most interesting to study the men and women who had taken the desperate chance and had won. Some of them had gone into the region with barely enough to keep body and soul together. They had only made the try as a last resort. Having failed to make success at home, they had resolved to make one plunge and die or come out rich. The most pathetic case of this kind was that of Mr. and Mrs. Berry. They went into the Klondike without even a grub-stake. They were on their wedding tour, and when they left they told their friends they might never get back to Fresno alive.

"This pair sat on the deck of the Portland fifteen months after their departure, and their plans embraced bigger things than scheming to find a man who would loan them $60 while they risked their lives trying to get over the mountains and into the placer district. They were like two children, Mr. Berry planning to buy the farm upon which he had been unable to make living wages, and Mrs. Berry getting ideas on the newest things in diamond rings. She had been forced to omit this feature of the ceremony when they started for Alaska, but like all women she was pleased that the ring could now be bought.

Gold in almost unlimited quantities

"It is evident from the conversation that I had with Mr. Berry and Mr. Phiscator that gold is going to be dug in Alaska in almost unlimited quantities. They were both a year in the centre of the gold fields — that is, the centre as it exists today. They were positive that the claims that had been staked out were only a small fraction of the claims that are going to pay big money. The prospectors in the district have not failed to find paying dirt in a single spot where a good search has been made. They said they had no idea how long or how wide the territory would prove to be, since no one has found the ends of the profitable veins.

"There are many claims along the best-known creeks that have been abandoned. The prospectors would be digging on them contentedly, earning big money every day. There would then come a report from some neighboring place of fabulously rich finds and there would follow at once a wild rush. In this way sites that paid moderately were passed in the search of others that would banish poverty in a month. The two kings of the region were wise enough to profit by the craze which carried the men along and they bought claim after claim along the Bonanza and the El Dorado. I do not think any man on earth can guess how much these men are worth today. They would be millionaires to stay at home the balance of their lives and sell interests in the mines they now have in operation.

Best mines still to be found

"Experts say that the best mines are still to be found. It is an old saying that the existence of the placer mine merely shows that not far away the mother rock must be found. It looks as if the gold in the loose dirt about the creeks had been brought down from the mountains by some great glacier. The men who have gone in and are going in have no capital for machinery and the placer mining is the only kind they can undertake. The late comers and the men with money for machinery will probably search for quartz veins and get bigger fortunes with but comparatively small expenditures. It is reported by government officials and everybody else that the whole country is gold producing and the work of 10,000 men who will be able to get there within the next twelve months will not begin to exhaust the resources.

Will try the overland route

"It is considerable of a venture for a woman to resolve to try to reach Dawson City by the overland route, but I think I can do it. We will start from Juneau the last of

April. Mrs. Berry went over the pass a year ago and I am anxious to have the experience. It is no easy task, but the dangers can be reduced to a minimum by wise preparations. The thing to do there, as every place else, is to do as the Romans do. It being a rather sensible conclusion that the Indians who have been following the trail for years and years have learned the best methods, I shall try to do very much as the Indians do.

How she will dress

"The weather at the beginning of the trip is likely to be very cold. I shall wear a bearskin hood and short skirts. There is then a serviceable garment, made of sealskin, with the fur inside. It serves as stockings. The shoes are moccasins made of rough leather, lined with thick woollen insoles. Snowshoes are indispensable for part of the way. Gloves of bearskin can be had from the natives and there is no storm that can penetrate the blankets of the Siwash Indians. We shall carry a small tent, trusting to the hemlock boughs for the beds.

"One of the hardships of the long tramp over the hills and along the frozen lakes comes from the lack of fresh meats. Game is scarce, and the Indians supply most of the moose and caribou. The flesh is frozen, and before it is cooked must be thawed out and cleaned. The natives have the crudest ideas of cleanliness. It takes some time to get accustomed to their ways, but necessity breeds forgiveness and forgetfulness as well. I fear nothing on the trip save the Chilkoot Pass, and at this time of year the chances are that we will have but little trouble. There will be much travel over it during the fall and coming winter, and the way will be greatly improved by the time we are ready to undertake it."

Chapter XII

The Climate

Those who go to the Klondike must prepare for cold weather

Neither those who think that Alaska is not so cold after all, nor those whose imagination pictures eight months of weather 90 degrees below zero are correct. At times the cold is intense, and of the winter of 1895-6, which was a severe one, Mr. William Ogilvie, the Dominion surveyor reports: "After my return there was sone fine clear weather in January, but it was exceedingly cold, more than 60 degrees below zero, one night 68.5 degrees, and as I had both my ears pretty badly frozen and could not go out in such cold without having them covered, so that I could not hear the chronometre beat, I could not observe until the end of the month, when we had two fine nights — 29th and 30th — mild enough for me to work."

United States report

A more exhaustive and complete statement of the climatic conditions of that region is contained in a United States Government report prepared under the direction of the Secretary of Agriculture by Willis L. Moore, Chief of the Weather Bureau. He says:

"The climates of the coast and interior of Alaska are unlike in many respects, and the differences are intensified in this, as perhaps in few other countries, by exceptional physical conditions. The fringe of islands that separates the mainland from the Pacific Ocean, from Dixon Sound north, and also a strip of the mainland for possibly twenty miles back from the sea, following the sweep of the coast as it curves to the northwestward to

the western extremity of Alaska, form a distinct climatic
division which may be termed temperate Alaska. The
temperature rarely falls to zero; winter does not set in
until December 1, and by the last of May the snow has
disappeared except on the mountains. The mean winter
temperature of Sitka is 32.5, but little less than that of
Washington, D.C.

"The rainfall of temperate Alaska is notorious the
world over, not only as regards the quantity, but also as
to the manner of its falling, viz., in long and incessant
rains and drizzles. Cloud and fog naturally abound, there
being on an average but sixty clear days in the year.

"North of the Aleutian Islands the coast climate
becomes more rigorous in winter, but in summer the
difference is much less marked.

Climate of the interior

"The climate of the interior, including that designation
practically all of the country except a narrow fringe of
coastal margin and the territory before referred to as
temperate Alaska, is one of extreme rigor in winter, with a
brief but relatively hot summer, especially when the sky is
free from cloud.

"In the Klondike region in midwinter the sun rises
from 9:30 to 10 a.m., and sets from 2 to 3 p.m., the total
length of daylight being about four hours. Remembering
that the sun rises but a few degrees above the horizon
and that it is wholly obscured on a great many days, the
character of the winter months may be easily imagined.

"We are indebted to the United States coast and
geodetic survey for a series of six months observations on
the Yukon, not far from the present site of the gold
discoveries. The observations were made with standard
instruments and are wholly reliable. The mean

temperatures of the months from October 1889, to April 1890, both inclusive, are as follows:

October	33
November	8
December	-11
January	-17
February	-15
March	6
April	20

"The daily mean temperature fell and remained below the freezing point (32 degrees) from Nov.4, 1889 to April 21, 1890, thus giving 168 days as the length of the closed season of 1889-90, assuming that outdoor operations are controlled by temperature only. The lowest temperatures registered during the winter were 32 degrees below zero in November, 47 below in December, 59 below in January, 55 below in February, 45 below in March, and 26 below in April. The greatest continuous cold occurred in February, 1890, when the daily mean for five consecutive days was 47 degrees below zero.

Has been colder in United States

"Greater cold than that here noted has been experienced in the United States for a very short time. In the interior of Alaska the winter sets in as early as September, when snowstorms may be expected in the mountains and passes. Headway during one of those storms is impossible, and the traveller who is overtaken by one of them is indeed fortunate if he escapes with his life. Snowstorms of great severity occur in any month from September to May inclusive.

"The changes of temperature from winter to summer are rapid, owing to the great increase in the length of the day. In May the sun rises at about 3 am and sets about 9 pm. In June it rises about 1:30 in the morning and sets at about 10:30 at night, giving about twenty hours of daylight and diffuse twilight the remainder of the time.

"The mean summer temperature in the interior doubtless ranges between 60 and 70 degrees, according to elevation, being highest in the middle and lower Yukon valleys."

Chapter XIII

Gold and its Distribution

Quartz and placers — how the gold came to the Klondike

Gold has been an object of interest to mankind from the earliest ages of civilization. In placers it is found almost pure, although seldom entirely so, and nearly every nugget contains some silver, copper or other metals. The gold from the Yukon is not as valuable as the product of California, the Klondike gold having from fifty to one hundred points more base metal. The base metals found in combination with this gold are iron, lead and silver, the iron giving the Yukon gold its fine, rich color. Of course these other metals decrease the value of the gold, which is about a dollar per ounce less than that of California gold. In the latter state nuggets run from $18 to $19 per ounce, and gold dust never less than $17 per ounce, while the Yukon product is valued at $17 to $18 per ounce for nuggets and $16 to $17 per ounce for gold dust.

Gold in mineral veins

While gold is distributed in many ways, its original state is in mineral veins, combined with various kinds of rocks, usually quartz, in bodies called "ledges" or "lodes" of varying width, between walls of stone of the surrounding formation, which is known as "country rock." These ledges are rarely perpendicular, but have a slanting direction, and the upper wall is therefore known as the "hanging wall" of the mine, the lower wall being the "foot wall". The quartz or other rock containing the gold and confined between the walls is called the "gangue".

Ore taken from a vein must be separated from the rock, and if the gold in it is not largely combined with base metals it is called "free milling ore" and the gold may be most easily procured by crushing the rock in a quartz mill, which is done by means of heavy stamps operated by power. When crushed as fine as possible it is transferred to pan amalgamators — large iron receptacles in which heavy iron grinders revolve, grinding the pulverised rock between flat surfaces until it becomes a fine mud, water being mingled with the mass. With this mixture quicksilver is used, the particles of gold adhering to the quicksilver and forming what is known as "amalgam". The dirt is washed from the amalgam in various ways, and then the latter is placed in a retort, which is heated until the quicksilver separates itself from the gold.

If the gold is in combination with other metals several processes are employed, such as smelting etc., and the resulting product is called "base bullion". Various chemical means have been employed to separate the gold from the baser metals, the agent used depending upon the minerals contained in the composite mass.

New reduction processes

Formerly the great expense in the extraction of gold from free milling ore consisted in the loss of mercury by what was called "flouring". When this occurred the particles of quicksilver lost their property of coalescing with and taking up the gold, and the frequent renewal of quicksilver made the cost heavy. It has, however, been discovered that this deterioration of the mercury can be almost completely prevented by the use of cyanide of potassium, and this cyanide process has greatly reduced the cost of procuring gold from ore, making it profitable to work mines which would be worthless if treated in the old way. Under any circumstances however, the mining of quartz is an expensive process, requiring capital and machinery, so that the prospectors whose means are

MINER EQUIPPED TO LOCATE GOLD

"All That Glitters Is Not Gold"

limited must, if they discover quartz mines, sell them, or an interest in them, to capitalists.

Gold in placers

In contra-distinction to the quartz mine is the placer mine, which is popularly called a "poor mans mine", because, if a paying claim is located, the owner can work it himself, needing nothing for success except a pick, shovel, pan, water and a supply of food.

Placer gold, in its various forms, is merely the waste of gold in ledges, separated and ground by volcanic, glacial or hydraulic action and finally deposited in alluvial soil, sand or gravel. The distribution of gold in veins is very wide, but on the continent of America is especially great in the Pacific Coast ranges of mountains which, in the broader sense, may be considered as one chain, extending from Patagonia to the Arctic Sea. Along the entire region of these mountains, including the Rocky Mountain and Sierra Nevada ranges in North America and the Andes and Cordilleras in South America, gold has been found at all points. Large deposits of alluvial gold indicate that at some period it has been ground out of the vein in which it belonged by some of nature's forces and transported by others. A strong geological theory is that all the various veins of gold-bearing quartz are more or less disconnected spurs of some great "mother lode" and that this lode exists in some part of the great Pacific chain. Von Humboldt believed that the mother vein would prove to be in Alaska, and the unprecedented richness of the deposits on the Klondike make that theory a most probable one.

Gold ground by glaciers

When glacial or other action has separated gold from the vein and begun its distribution, the remainder of the work is done by the action of water. The mountain streams, swollen to rapid action by rain or melted snow, carry along dirt, sand and gravel with the gold. The gravel and gold settle on the bottom of the creek and above that sand and dirt in which a comparatively small amount of gold may be found. Usually the largest amount of gold is in the gravel bottom, central to the course of the stream, but in the settling, bars may have been formed by the heavier stones in the gravel, which have caught the gold in especially large quantities, these rich masses being known as "pockets", and there may be crevices in the bedrock, in which case these are most likely receptacles for deposits of gold. When the gold is carried along by the force of water its great weight causes it to sink as soon as the impelling force of the water relaxes sufficiently to allow the law of gravitation to work. The coarser particles are left high up the stream, the finer ones travelling further and being deposited in the bed or bars of the lower creek or river. Subsequent floods or freshets repeat the operation of distributing the gold, and the final result is extensive deposits of gold in gravel, sand and earth in gulches, creeks and rivers.

Nuggets and dust

Gold lumps of about half an ounce or more are called "nuggets;" when the particles are fine they are called "dust;" and sizes between these two are designated as "coarse gold," the latter frequently being interspersed with nuggets.

The gold workings on the Bonanza and Eldorado creeks in the Klondike region are of coarse gold. In this rich district not only in the gravel next to bedrock, but also above in the finer clay and sand, gold is found in paying quantities.

Chapter XIV

Working Placer Mines

How gold is taken from the ground in the Klondike district

In the Klondike region a very peculiar system of mining is in vogue. The ground is frozen from the bedrock to the surface in the winter, and never thaws out to any great depth. The surface is covered with glacial mud, upon which there is a thick mass of moss. The top of the ground is so thickly felted with this moss that the latter acts as an insulation, preventing the warm rays of the 24 hour sun from thawing the ground even in the summer.

The top "muck" as it is called by the miners, is, when thawed out, about two thirds water and one third sediment. Its large percentage of moisture makes it impossible to thaw it out with fire satisfactorily, so this portion has to be removed with a pick or blasted off. The latter process is, however, rarely employed because of a scarcity of powder, so that it is usually removed with a pick.

Thawing out the ground

After this murky top layer is cleaned off the method is to build a huge fire, probably two feet wide and six or eight feet long. After this has burned six or eight hours the ground beneath it is thawed sufficiently so that five or six inches of dirt can be taken out. This operation is repeated, and it is found that the deeper one goes the more readily the ground thaws.

The shafts are sunk until bedrock is reached. That is the bottom of the deposit, and on Bonanza creek it is encountered at a depth of all the way from three to 20 feet. The pay streak is often 150 feet wide, and when bedrock is reached what is technically called "burning a breast" is

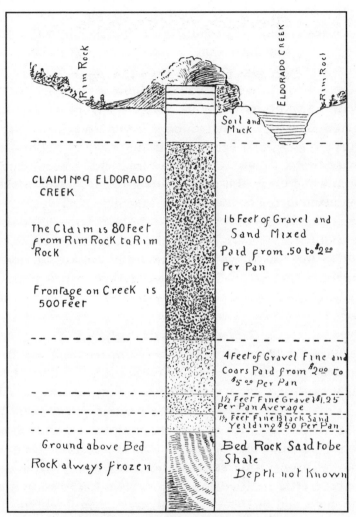

DIAGRAM OF GOLD CLAIM ON EL DORADO CREEK
$40,000 was taken from the shaft alone.

restored to. That, in plain English, consists of running a tunnel on a level through the pay streak.

The ground is much more easily thawed in these tunnels, and it not infrequently happens that one burning thaws out fifteen feet.

Plenty of wood for burning

There is an ample supply of wood in the Klondike region, so that little difficulty has been experienced on that score, the maximum distance of wood from the mine being about three-quarters of a mile and most claims being much nearer than that to a good supply.

As soon as the dirt is thawed out it is hauled to the surface and piled upon the dump. When the thawing weather arrives and the water comes down, the "sluicing" begins and the gold is washed from the gravel and dirt by the usual methods, hereafter described.

The methods of mining in the winter have only been introduced into the Yukon during recent years and constitute the novelty in the mining methods of that region as compared with those in vogue elsewhere.

The prospector's outfit

In prospecting for mines the outfit required, besides food and cooking utensils, includes a pan, light pick, shovel and axe, and a machete for cutting out underbrush and other purposes will also be found of value. Creeks and gulches are tried in order to find gold, which is done by experimental digging and panning. As only one claim is allowed to each person on one creek (except that the discoverer is entitled to twice as much ground as the others) it is a matter of great importance to locate in the best ground possible.

Locating the claim

The amount of ground one person may take is limited by general law as to the maximum, and may not be exceeded. Miners' regulations may reduce the amount, but all are to be treated alike in the same district. Claims

TOOLS AND IMPLEMENTS OF PLACER MINERS

are numbered from the "Discovery Claim" consecutively — "No. 1 above" or "No. 1 below", etc. Thus, Clarence J. Berry's claim is described as "No. 5 above Discovery, El Dorado Creek."

When located the ground should be measured off and staked and the locator is entitled, in the Klondike region, to 500 feet along the creek, and from rim to rim, the rim being the point on either bank where the "pay dirt" terminates or the bedrock emerges above the surface.

Washing out the gold

After the dirt is taken out and when the water comes in the early summer, the washing out process commences. The primitive mode is to use a pan, which is large enough to hold two shovelfuls of dirt and allow for a bucketful or so of water. The dirt is washed by letting that which rises to the top drain off. The pan is shaken gently, water added as required, and the washing is kept up until most of the soluble portion has washed away. From time to time, as the water drains out, the operator looks at the residuum. Finally a gleam of yellow is seen at the bottom.

The pan shows "color!"

So the miner designates it, and a most exciting thing is this looking for the "color" when prospecting for new mines.

Taking out the gold

After the color shows, the final washing is given and the coarse gravel picked out, while the finer sand washes away. The "dust" secured is put away in the sack. Sometimes a smaller pan is used for the final washing.

On a larger scale other appliances are used. One of these is the cradle, so called because it is mounted on rockers to give it the required motion. It has a movable hopper with a perforated bottom, or "riddle plate," of sheet

PANNING OUT GOLD ON THE KLONDIKE

iron, in which the "pay dirt" is placed. Water is poured on the dirt, and the rocking motion imparted to the cradle causes the finer particles to pass through the holes on to a canvas screen, and thence to the base of the cradle, which is crossed by bars of wood called riffles which catch the auriferous particles.

Another device is the "tom," a kind of cradle which has a perforated riddle placed immediately over the "riffle box," and has the riffles arranged on an inclined plane, the inclination being one foot in twelve. The riffle box of the "tom" is longer than that of the common cradle.

"Sluicing out" gold

For larger washings the method is by sluicing. The "sluice boxes" are troughs about 12 feet long, 12 to 20 inches wide and 12 inches deep. They are made tapering so as to be joined in series, and the total length depends upon the

"ROCKING OUT" GOLD ON THE KLONDIKE

amount and shape of the ground, but often runs several hundred feet. The size of the sluice boxes should be regulated by the width of the available lumber, as it is not desirable to have the bottom made of more than one width of plank.

The sluice boxes are placed at an incline varying from one in eight to one in sixteen. The floor of the boxes is laid with riffles, or pieces of 2 x 2 lumber laid parallel with the side and with notched planks laid transversely. These riffles catch the auriferous particles and are panned out at regular intervals, the "clean up" ordinarily being made once a week,

MINE IN KLONDIKE REGION
Showing sluice boxes in place

but oftener where the ground is very rich — sometimes daily.

If the gold is very fine, mercury is used above the notched planks to catch the minute particles and the amalgam thus formed is separated in the ordinary way, as described in the account of quartz milling.

There are numerous other ways of working gold, but they are only used by companies operating on a large scale, and are not in vogue in the Yukon districts.

Preparations for mining

Before beginning to work the claim it is necessary to build a house and to prepare for winter. In all of the Klondike region logs are plentiful. They should be well squared so as to make the interstices between the logs as small as possible, and the cracks should be well filled with the moss which grows all around. The roof is made of poles placed close together, then covered with moss, with a layer of dirt above. It can be so securely felted in this way as to make a tight and comfortable roof.

Fitting up the cabin

The interior of the cabin will be fitted up according to the ability of the occupant. A small sash will be required for light, and another outside sash will be needed in the winter. If the miner can not afford a floor he goes without. If he has any luck with hunting, a few skins on the floor make excellent rugs. Hemlock boughs, which are plentiful, make a good bed for one who is "roughing it," and keep the body away from the dampness of the ground. Of course the sheet-iron stove is a necessity of the cabin, and a good supply of wood for winter is one of the things to look out for.

For the meats which one does not care to keep in the house a "cache" should be built. For Master Bruin (to say nothing of foxes and wolves) is likely to come around when all is quiet and claim a share of the provender.

Winter work

In the winter much work can be done underground. It is not necessary to work long at a time above the ground in hauling the dirt to the surface to be dumped; and below ground it is much warmer, because there one is sheltered from cold wind. Our miner will need a lantern, because in the winter an hour or two of daylight is the most that can be hoped for.

Night in the camp

The hours of work can be regulated to suit the conditions. At night, when the Aurora Borealis is flashing and scintillating in the north, the best place is the inside of the cabin, where with his partner (every miner should have a partner), the prospective millionaire can tell his day dreams, or if he has a book, can read. If he wants a drink of cheering stuff he will find coffee or tea the best. Under any conditions of work or idleness whisky is the worst thing a Yukoner can drink in either the summer or winter climate of that country, and surest bar to the success of the hopes he brought with him.

Chapter XV

The Law and the Miner

How the prospector must proceed to get his claim

Part of the Yukon region is in the territory of the United States and part in that of Canada. There seems to be an idea abroad that there is a boundary dispute in regard to the ownership of the recently discovered mines in the Klondike region, but there is none.

Disputed boundary

There is a difference of claims in regard to the title to the lands in the vicinity of Dyea, Juneau and the coastline of Alaska west to the 141st degree of longitude. It is admitted that the United States took all the title that Russia had, but the dispute is as to where the line runs. If the United States claim should be upheld the line crosses Alsek river and crosses the northeast end of Chilkoot Pass at the head of Lake Lindermann, a small lake to the south of Lake Bennett, and thence runs southeast. The British claim that the line runs from Mount St. Elias down to Glacier Bay, crosses Muir Glacier peninsula and Lynn Canal, and runs back of Juneau only a few miles, taking in St. Mary's Island, on which there is a United States custom house. This dispute will probably be settled without friction, as it is a question of construction to be placed on a legal document and only affects the Klondike matter by its bearing on the route to the mines, because the British claim takes in Dyea and Chilkoot Pass.

Klondike is in Canada

As to the Klondike region itself there is no dispute. The line's the 141st degree of west longitude, and Dawson City is more than a full degree to the east of it. There are rich

PROSPECTORS' CAMP ON THE KLONDIKE

gold bearing streams on the American side of the line, and some of these creeks, like Forty-Mile, have their head in American and their mouth in British territory. But so far as the Klondike region is concerned the American miner going in will have to submit to Canadian law, some parts of which are very good, while the remainder is very arbitrary.

Must pay duty

On the route to the mines the miner who goes in with goods bought in the United States will be subject to the customs laws of the Dominion, the Canadian government having appointed D.W. Davis customs officer for the district embracing the Northwest Territory.

Law in Dawson City

When the prospector arrives in Dawson City he will find two authorities who are in their special departments

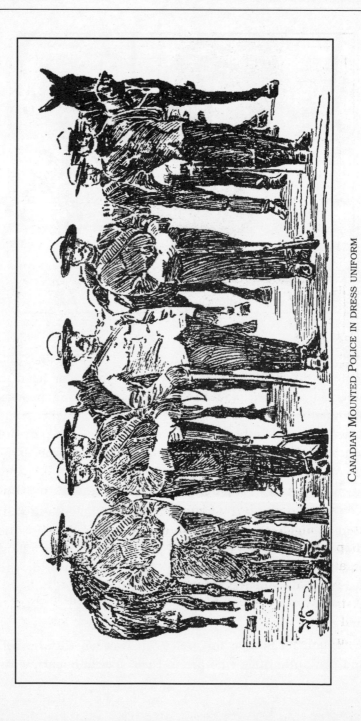

CANADIAN MOUNTED POLICE IN DRESS UNIFORM

CANADIAN MOUNTED POLICE

supreme. One is the Mounted Police, having charge of the law and order of the district, pursuing a liberal policy but keeping excesses well in hand. The other is the Gold Commissioner, who, under Canadian law, has charge of the administration of the mining laws, the settlement of disputed claims, and in fact, all that pertains to the location, entry, working and title to mines.

In regard to the maintenance of law and order in the district the Dominion government has recently decided to add eighty men to the twenty already on the force of the Mounted Police.

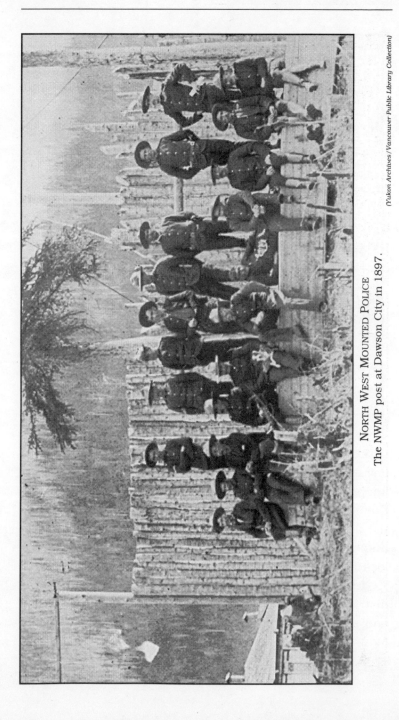

NORTH WEST MOUNTED POLICE
The NWMP post at Dawson City in 1897.

(Yukon Archives/Vancouver Public Library Collection)

POLICE POST

View of 1897 police barracks, surrounded by a wooden palisade

(Yukon Archives / National Museum of Canada Collection)

Police officers magistrates

The officers of each detachment of police will be appointed stipendary magistrates, so that means will be furnished for the administration of law and order promptly and satisfactorily. A strong customs and police post will be established a short distance north of the 60th degree of latitude, just above the northern boundary of British Columbia, and beyond the head of the Lynn Canal, where the Chilkoot Pass and the White Pass converge. This post will command the southern entrance to the whole of that territory. A strong detachment of police will be stationed there, and the necessary barrack accommodations will be erected. Further on small police posts will be established, about fifty miles apart, up to Fort Selkirk.

Telegraph line projected

If it is possible to construct a telegraph line from the head of the Lynn Canal over the mountains to the first post just north of the British Columbia boundary, it would overcome the great present drawback of lack of means of winter communication with the Klondike. It is accordingly the intention of the government to ascertain the probable cost of the construction of such a line, and if the project is found to be feasible, to put it into execution. The government proposes also at once to get the approximate cost of a wagon road and of a narrow gauge railroad over the territory between the coast and the post beyond the mountains. The provisions of the Real Property Act of the Northwest Territories will be extended to the Yukon country by an order in council, a Register will be appointed, and a land title office will be established.

Royalty to be paid

The question of the amount of the royalty which the Dominion government will exact from all ore taken from the soil has also been decided upon. This royalty will be 10 per cent on all amounts taken out of any one claim up to $500 a month, and after that 20 per cent. This royalty will be collected on gold taken from teams already being worked, but in regard to all future discoveries the government proposes that upon every river and creek where mining locations shall be staked out every alternative claim shall be the property of the government.

Fees for the Canadian government

The last provision is an addition to the already established charge of $15 registration fee and $100 annual rental already being collected under the laws now in force. It is a most stringent and illiberal provision, excelling in its severity any ever before imposed in either British or United States Territory. It is in especially strong contrast to the policy that has always characterised the dealings of the United States with those who have braved frontier dangers in the development of the mining regions. There is no discrimination in the new regulations between Canadians and others, but the extortionate imposts oppress all alike.

The following are the laws of Canada pertaining to the location of mines in the Northwest Territory of Canada, and applicable in the Klondike District.

PLACER MINING
REGISTRATION AND FEES

At the close of the second sitting of the Canadian cabinet recently it was announced that the government had decided to impose a royalty on all placer diggings on the Yukon in addition to $15 registration fee and $100 annual assessment. The royalty will be 10 per cent each on claims with an output of $500 or less monthly, and 20 per cent on every claim yielding above that amount monthly. Besides this royalty it has been decided, in regard to all future claims staked out on other streams or rivers, that every alternate claim should be the property of the government, and should be reserved for public purposes and sold or worked by the government for the benefit of the revenue of the dominion.

NATURE AND SIZE OF CLAIMS

For "bar diggings" — a strip of land 100 feet wide at high water mark, and thence extending into the river at its lowest water level.

For "dry diggings" — one hundred feet square.

For "creek and river claims" — five hundred feet along the direction of the stream, extending in width from base to base of the hill or bench on either side. The width of such claims, however, is limited to 600 feet when the benches are a greater distance apart than that. In such a case claims are laid out in areas of ten acres, with boundaries running north and south, east and west.

For "bench claims" — one hundred feet square.

Size of claims to discoverers or parties of discoverers, to one discoverer — 300 feet in length; to a party of two, 600 feet in length; to a party of three, 800 feet in length; to a party of four 1,000 feet in length; to a party of more than four, ordinary sized claims only.

New strata of auriferous gravel in a locality where claims are abandoned, or dry diggings, or *vice versa*, shall be deemed new mines.

RIGHTS AND DUTIES OF MINERS

Entries of grants for placer mining must be renewed and entry fees paid every year.

No miner shall received more than one claim in the same locality, but may hold any number of claims by purchase, and any number of miners may unite to work their claims in common, provided an agreement be duly registered and a registration fee of $5 be duly paid therefore.

Claims may be mortgaged or disposed of, provided such disposal be registered and a registration fee of $2 be paid therefore.

Although miners shall have exclusive right of entry upon their claims for the "miner-like" working of them, holders of adjacent claims shall be granted such right of entry thereon as may seem reasonable to the superintendent of mines.

Each miner shall be entitled to so much of the water not previously appropriated flowing through or past his claim as the superintendent of mines shall deem necessary to work it, and shall be entitled to drain his own claim free of charge.

Claims remaining unworked on working days for seventy-two hours are deemed abandoned, unless sickness or other reasonable cause is shown or unless the grantee is absent on leave.

For the convenience of miners on back claims, on benches or slopes, permission may be granted by the superintendent of mines to tunnel through claims fronting on water course.

In case of the death of a miner, the provisions of abandonment do not apply during his last illness or after his decease.

ACQUISITION OF MINING LOCATIONS
MARKING LOCATIONS

Wooden posts 4 inches square, driven 18 inches into the ground and projecting 18 inches above it, must mark the four corners of a location. In rocky ground stone mounds 3 feet in diameter may be piled about the post. In timbered land well blazed lines must join the posts. In rolling or uneven localities flattened posts must be placed at intervals along the lines to mark them, so that subsequent explorers shall have no trouble in tracing such lines. When locations are bounded by lines running north and south, east and west, the stake at the northeast corner shall be marked by a cutting instrument or by coloured chalk, "M.L. No. 1" (mining location, stake number 1). Likewise the southeasterly stake shall be marked "M.L. No. 2," the southwesterly "M.L. No. 3" and the northwesterly "M.L. No. 4." Where the boundary lines do not run north and south, east and west, the northerly stake shall be marked 1, the easterly 2, the southerly 3 and the westerly 4. On each post shall be marked also the claimant's initials and the distance to the next post.

APPLICATION AND AFFIDAVIT OF DISCOVERER

Within sixty days after making his location the claimant shall file in the office of the dominion land office for the district a formal declaration, sworn to before the land agent, describing as nearly as may be the locality and dimensions of the location. With such declaration he must pay the agent an entry fee of $5.

RECEIPT ISSUED TO DISCOVERER

Upon such payment the agent shall grant a receipt authorizing the claimant, or his legal representative, to enter into possession, subject to renewal every year for five years, provided that in these five years $100 shall be expended on the claim in actual mining operations. A detailed statement of such expenditure must also be filed with the agent of dominion lands, in the form of an affidavit corroborated by two reliable and disinterested witness.

ANNUAL RENEWAL OF LOCATION CERTIFICATE

Upon payment of the $5 fee therefore a receipt shall be issued entitling the claimant to hold the location for another year.

WORKING IN PARTNERSHIP

Any party of four or less neighbouring miners, within three months after entering, may, upon being authorized by the agent, make upon any one of such locations, during the first and second years, but not subsequently, the expenditure otherwise required on each of the locations. An agreement, however, accompanied by a fee of $5 must be filed with the agent. Provided, however, that the expenditure made upon any one location shall not be applicable in any manner or for any purpose to any other location.

PURCHASE OF LOCATION

At any time before the expiration of five years from date of entry a claimant may purchase a location upon filing with the agent proof that he has expended $500 in actual mining operations on the claim and complied with all other prescribed regulations. The price of a mining location shall be $5 per acre, cash.

On making an application to purchase, the claimant must deposit with the agent $50 to be deemed as payment to the government for the survey of his location. On receipt of plans and field notes and approval by the surveyor-general a patent shall issue to the claimant.

REVERSION OF TITLE

Failure of a claimant to prove within each year the expenditure prescribed, or failure to pay the agent the full cash price, shall cause the claimant's right to lapse and the location to revert to the crown, along with the improvements upon it.

RIVAL CLAIMANTS

When two or more persons claim the same location, the right to acquire it shall be in him who can prove he was the first to discover the mineral deposit involved, and to take possession in the prescribed manner. Priority of discovery alone, however shall not give the right to acquire. A subsequent discoverer, who has complied with other prescribed conditions, shall take precedence over a prior discoverer who has failed so to comply.

When a claimant has in bad faith used the prior discovery of another and has fraudulently affirmed that he made independent discovery and demarcation, he shall, apart from other legal consequences, have no claim forfeit his deposit and be absolutely debarred from obtaining another location.

RIVAL APPLICANTS

Where there are two or more applicants for a mining location, neither of whom is the original discoverer, the minister of the interior may invite competitive tenders or put it up for public auction, as he sees fit.

TRANSFER OF MINING RIGHTS
ASSIGNMENT OF RIGHT TO PURCHASE

An assignment of the right to purchase a location shall be endorsed on the back of the receipt or certificate of assignment, and execution thereof witnessed by two disinterested witnesses. Upon the deposit of such receipt in the office of the land agent, accompanied by a registration fee of $2, the agent shall give the assignee a certificate entitling him to all the rights of the original discoverer. By complying with the prescribed regulations such assignee becomes entitled to purchase the location.

QUARTZ MINING

Regulations in respect to placer mining, so far as they relate to entries, entry fees, assignments, marking of locations, agents receipts, etc. except where otherwise provided, apply also to quartz mining.

NATURE AND SIZE OF CLAIMS

A location shall not exceed the following dimensions; Length, 1,500 feet; breadth, 600 feet. The surface boundaries shall be from straight parallel lines, and its boundaries beneath the surface the planes of these lines.

LIMIT TO NUMBER OF LOCATIONS

Not more than one mining location shall be granted to any one individual claiming upon the same lode or vein.

MILL SITES

Land used for milling purposes may be applied for and patented, either in connection with or separate from a mining location, and may be held in addition to a mining location, provided such additional land shall in no case exceed five acres.

GENERAL PROVISIONS

DECISION OF DISPUTES

The superintendent of mines shall have power to hear and determine all disputes in regard to mining property arising within his district, subject to appeal by either of the parties to the commissioner of dominion lands.

LEAVE OF ABSENCE

Each holder of a mining location shall be entitled to be absent and suspend work on his diggings during the "close" season, which "close" season shall be declared by the agent in each district, under instructions from the minister of the interior.

The agent may grant a leave of absence pending the decision of any dispute before him.

Any miner is entitled to a year's leave of absence upon proving expenditure of not less than $200 without any reasonable return of gold.

The time occupied by a locator in going to and returning from the office of the agent or of the superintendent of mines shall not count against him.

ADDITIONAL LOCATIONS

The minister of the interior may grant to a person actually developing a location an adjoining location equal in size, provided it be shown to the minister's satisfaction that the vein being worked will probably extend beyond the boundaries of the original location.

FORFEITURE

In event of the breach of the regulations, a right or grant shall be absolutely forfeited, and the offending party shall be incapable of subsequently acquiring similar rights, except by special permission by the minister of the interior.

UNITED STATES MINING LAW

Those who locate upon the American side of the line, which includes the rich Birch Creek mines, the mines on the headwaters of Sixty-Mile and Forty-Mile Creeks, the American Creek, the Tanana River and a vast number of other streams, will find their rights and privileges well set forth in the following synopsis, which was prepared by Charles M. Walter for the Chicago *Times Herald*:

PLACER CLAIM DEFINED

The term placer claim as defined by the supreme court of the United States is "Ground within defined boundaries which contains mineral in its earth, sand or gravel; ground that includes valuable deposits not in place, that is, not fixed in rock, but which are in a loose state, and may in most cases be collected by washing or amalgamation without milling."

SIZE OF QUARTZ AND PLACER CLAIMS

The manner of locating placer mining claims differs from that of locating claims upon veins or lodes. In locating a vein or lode claim the United States Statues provide that no claim shall extend more than 300 feet on each side of the middle of the vein at the surface, and that no claim shall be limited by mining regulations to less than 25 feet on each side of the middle of the vein at the surface. In locating claims called placers, however, the law provides that no location of such claim upon surveyed lands shall include more than twenty acres for each individual claimant. The supreme court, however, has held that one individual can hold as many locations as he can purchase and rely upon his possessory title; that a separate patent for each location is unnecessary.

PROOF OF CITIZENSHIP

Locators, however have to show proof of citizenship or intention to become citizens. This may be done in the case of an individual by his own affidavit; in the case of an association incorporated by a number of individuals by the affidavit of their authorized agent, made on his own knowledge or upon information and belief; and in the case of a company organized under the laws of any state or territory by the filing of a certified copy of the character or certificate of incorporation.

PATENTS

A patent for any land claimed and located may be obtained in the following manner: "Any person, association or corporation authorized to locate a claim, having claimed and located a piece of land, and who has or have complied with the terms of the law, may file in the proper land office an application for a patent under oath, showing such compliance, together with a plat and field notes of the claim or claims in common made by or under the direction of the United States surveyor general, showing accurately the boundaries of the claim or claims, which shall be distinctly marked by monuments on the ground, and shall post a copy of such plat, together with a notice of such application for a patent in a conspicuous place on the land embraced in such plat, previous to the application for a patent on such plat; and shall file an affidavit of at least two persons that such notice has been duly posted, and shall file a copy of the notice in such land office; and shall thereupon be entitled to a patent to the land in the manner following: The registrar of said land office upon the filing of such application, plat, field notes, notices and affidavits shall publish a notice that such application has been made, for a period of sixty days, in a newspaper to be by him designated, as published nearest to such claim; and he shall post such notice in his office for the same period. The claimant at the time of filing such application or at any time thereafter, within sixty days of publication, shall file with the registrar a certificate of the Unties States surveyor general that $500 worth of labour has been expended or improvements made upon the claim by himself or grantors; that the plat is correct, with such further description by reference to natural objects or permanent monuments as shall identify the claim and furnish an accurate description to be incorporated in the patent. At the expiration of the sixty days of publication, the claimant shall file his affidavit showing that the plat and notice have been posted in a conspicuous place on the claim during such period of publication."

ADVERSE CLAIMS

If no adverse claim shall have been filed with the registrar of the land office at the expiration of said sixty days, the claimant is entitled to a patent upon the payment to the proper officer of $5 per acre in the case of a lode claim, and $2.50 per acre for a placer.

The location of a placer claim and keeping possession thereof until a patent shall be issued are subject to local laws and customs.

LAWS APPLICABLE TO ALASKA

Many misunderstandings have arisen in regard to the land and mineral laws applicable to Alaska, some of the United States laws being, by explicitly enactment, not operative in the district of Alaska. The Commissioner of the General Land Office has recently published a statement which shows that these are the laws applicable to Alaska:

(1) The mineral land laws of the United States; (2) town site laws, which provide for the incorporation of town sites and acquirement of title thereto from the United States Government to the town site Trustees; (3) the laws providing for trade and manufacturers, giving each qualified person 160 acres of land in a square and

compact form. The coal land regulations are distinct from the mineral regulations or laws, and the jurisdiction of neither coal laws nor public land laws extends to Alaska, the Territory being expressly excluded by the laws themselves from their operation. The act approved May 17, 1884, providing for civil government for Alaska, has this language as to mines and mining privileges:

"The laws of the United States relating to mining claims and rights incidental thereto shall on and after the passage of this act be in full force and effect in said district of Alaska, subject to such regulations as may be made by the Secretary of the Interior and approved by the President," and "parties who have located mines or mining privileges therein, under the United States laws, applicable to the public domain, or have occupied or improved or exercised acts of ownership over such claims shall not be disturbed therein, but shall be allowed to perfect title by payment so provided for." There is still more general authority.

Without this special authority the act of July 4, 1886, says: "All valuable mineral deposits in lands belonging to the United States, both surveyed and unsurveyed, are hereby declared to be free and open to exploration and purchase, and lands in which these are found to occupations and purchase by citizens of the United States and by those who have declared an intention to become such under the rules prescribed by law and according to local customs or rules of miners in the several mining districts, so far as the same are applicable and not inconsistent with the laws of the United States."

The patenting of mineral lands in Alaska is not a new thing, for that work has been going on, as the cases have come in from time to time since 1884.

Chapter XVI

Alaska

Facts about the land of ice, seals and gold

A sudden interest has sprung up in the United States in regard to the great land which, although owned by this country for thirty years, has received but little general attention.

Seals and totem poles

Alaska has, to the general reader, been principally known as a land of seals and totem poles — the seals being with us always as a subject to quarrel over and be arbitrated. For a long time Alaska was looked upon as a good joke, and Secretary Seward's purchase of the country from the Russians was freely and keenly ridiculed as a piece of useless extravagance only to be condoned in consideration of the friendly sympathy which Russia had shown to the Union cause during the Civil War. So the matter was allowed to drop as a subject of discussion, and the allusions to "Uncle Sam's Ice Box," as the country had been called, became infrequent. Later it became the fashion for tourists to take a brief trip to the southern coast of Alaska to see the glaciers and other scenery, while the country north of the coast range remained a *terra incognita* unknown and unheeded.

Discovery of Alaska

Alaska came into the possession of the United States by purchase in 1867, the price paid being $7,200,000 in gold. Before that it had been know as Russian America, having come into the possession of Russia by right of discovery, the first Europeans to see the Alaskan shores having been the Russian navigator, Vitus Bering, who was a Dane by birth but was in the service of the Russian government. He sailed east from Kamchatka, reaching the American shore in 1728. Bering made several voyages and was the first European to sail on the waters now known as Bering Sea and Bering Strait.

Russian Dominion

The explorations of Bering were followed by many voyages by Siberian fur hunters, who took control of the Aleutian islands and enslaved the natives, treating the latter with such severity that their numbers decreased 90 per cent in the sixty years prior to 1818.

The Russian American company was organized in 1799, and received from the Emperor Paul, a charter. Their manager, Baranoff, conquered the country as far as Sitka, which was founded in 1801; established a colony in California, and engaged in commerce with China, Hawaii and the Spanish colonies of the Pacific main. He established the seat of government at Unalaska and was a man of iron, cruel and despotic. The Russian government interfered on behalf of the natives in 1818 and their enslavement ceased, the Christianizing efforts of the missionary Innocentius Veniaminoff, afterward primate of the Greek Church, resulting in the conversion of thousands of Aleuts and other natives.

Natives badly treated

Although some of the grosser features of oppression were eliminated after the imperial intervention in 1818, the natives received very bad treatment during the entire period of Russian occupation, the fur company having no object in the country except to enrich itself. Its barbarous treatment of the natives at the various trading posts established became such a scandal that upon the expiry of its charter in 1862 the government refused further renewal.

Under the stars and stripes

After the negotiations of purchase were completed with Russia in 1867 the Russian standard was lowered and the stars and stripes unfurled on the barracks at Sitka and from Russian America the name of the country was changed to "Alaska." The names of "Polaio," "American Siberia," "Zero Islands" and "Walrussia" were suggested, but Charles Sumner advocated the name "Alaska" from the aboriginal Al-ak-shak meaning "the great country" or "the continent."

Size of Alaska

Alaska has an area of 531,400 square miles, equalling one sixth of the United States or one seventh of Europe, and being twice as large as Texas, the largest of the American States. It presents great varieties of climate. Southern Alaska, under the influence of the Japan stream which flows by it, having its climate moderated so that it has no great extremes of heat and cold, the mean temperature of Sitka being 54.2 degrees in summer and 31.9 degrees in winter. That part of the country is very humid and the rainfall is from 80 to 130 inches in a year.

General characteristics

The general characteristics of the interior have been elsewhere described in the chapter on the Yukon Valley and the special one on the climate of the country. In Southeastern Alaska there are large forests, the principal tree being the Sitka spruce, which not infrequently reaches the height of 250 feet and covers thousands of square miles of the Alexander archipelago. Yellow cedar, a wood admitting of high polish and having a pleasant, perfumed odour, is one of the many excellent trees of this region.

The Alaskan coast line

The coast of Southeastern Alaska curves northward and westward from Dixon Entrance to Prince William Sound 550 miles and from there the shore-line extends southward and westward for 725 miles to the tip of Alaska. From that point the coast line takes a zigzag northward course to Bering Strait and the Arctic Ocean.

The Aleutian Islands

From the southwestern peninsula extends out into the ocean the Aleutian islands, dividing Bering Sea from the Pacific main. This archipelago extends for over 1,650 miles in the direction of Asia and is composed of treeless, grassy, mountainous islands, around which blow storms which make the name of the Pacific seem a hollow mockery, while the overhanging mists testify to the humidity of the climate. The moderating influence of the ocean stream that flows by these islands is shown by a temperature which averages 50 degrees in summer and 30 degrees in winter.

Our ultimate west and north

The island of Attu is the most westerly point of the United States, and is situated 400 miles east of Kamchatka and 400 miles west of the nearest Alaskan village. It rises to a height of 3,084 feet and is the home of about 140 Aleuts. This island is 2,943 miles west of San Francisco, or a little further than the distance (2,900 miles) between the latter city and the most eastern point in Maine. The most northerly point in the United States is Point Barrow, where there is a building erected by the government and a relief station. It is maintained as a trading and relief point; many whalers being lost at this dangerous coast. Near the point is the Eskimo village of Nuwak.

Rivers of Alaska

The principal river of Alaska is the Yukon, which is fully described elsewhere. It enters American territory between Fort Cudahy (Forty-Mile) and Circle City and empties into Norton Sound. Its principal tributary in United States territory is the Tanana which joins the main river at Weare.

The Kuskokwim River and the Nootak River, the former emptying into Bering Sea and the latter into the Arctic Ocean north of Bering Strait are both long rivers whose tributary branches and creeks are said to be rich in gold. The climate and other conditions along these rivers are about the same as those on the Yukon.

The Copper River, which empties into the Pacific to the west of Mount Elias, has been explored by several parties, including Lieutenant Schwatka, who came out from the Yukon by way of White and Copper rivers. The river is little known but is regarded as one of the more promising prospecting grounds. It has been said that a route by the Copper River could be made to the Klondike country which would reduce the distance to not more than 300 miles from the coast.

Proposed route to Klondike

The proposed route starts inland from the mouth of Copper River which it follows up to the mouth of its principal tributary, the Chillyna River, which is navigable for a considerable distance. From the head of the Chillyna a short road over a low pass would, it is said, reach White River, a navigable stream entering the Yukon between Fort Selkirk and the mouth of Stewart River.

Gold at many points

Gold has been found at many places in Alaska besides the Yukon, and on Cook's inlet a number of placer mines are being successfully worked. Mr. George F. Beecher, in an unpublished report made to the geological survey of his investigation in 1895 of the coastal gold districts, says that most of the islands of the Alexander archipelago contain gold deposits, yet unworked, that would probably repay very handsomely well-directed efforts of placer mining.

These deposits are in the neighborhood of Sitka and generally on Baranoff and Admiralty islands and the beaches of the adjacent mainland.

Another fairly promising region is in a group of deposits on the Kenai peninsula, on the southeast shore of Cook inlet and at Yakutal bay and the beaches of Kadiak island.

These regions have as yet been exploited only to a limited degree, owing to the unfavorable physical condition of the coast.

The natives of Alaska

The ethnological features of Alaska are very interesting, the Eskimos of the north and west; the Aleuts, a Mongolian race inhabiting the Aleutian archipelago; the Tlingits of Southeastern Alaska and the various Indian tribes of the interior all being races of great interest to the scientific investigator. The aboriginals of the Upper Yukon are the Takudh or Takuth Indians, although they always speak of themselves as Yukon

Indians. Their language is known to missionaries as a dialect of Takudh, but they converse with traders in a jargon call "Slavey," a mixture of Canadian French and hybrid words of English.

Mountains of Alaska

The Alaskan mountains reach magnificent proportions and are the highest mountains north of Mexico. Mt. St. Elias is 18,200 feet high; Mt. Wrangell, and active volcano, 19,400 feet; Mt. Crillon, 15,900 feet; and Mt. Fairweather, 15,500 feet, being among the most lofty. Alaska is famous for its glaciers, which number thousands along the southern coast line. The Muir glacier, on its sea front, is three miles long, and presents a great wall of blue ice 350 feet high, with a background of mountains 15,000 feet high. There are numerous glaciers between Juneau and Chilkoot Pass on the way to the Klondike region.

Seal fisheries

The seal fisheries of Alaska are famous, and the plant of the Russian-American Company was in 1870 bought by the Alaskan Commercial Company, composed of San Francisco capitalists, who continued the seal fisheries under a twenty-years' charter. In 1890 the lease of the fur seal islands passed into the hands of the North American Commercial Company.

The breeding grounds are on the Pribyloff Islands in Bering Sea and regulations are now in force to prevent the destruction of the seals at a greater rate than their natural annual increase.

Fish in Alaskan seas

The fisheries of Alaska are of great and growing value, and the salmon canning industry is one of large importance. Codfish, halibut and other valuable food fish abound in Alaskan waters, which are destined to become a most prolific source of supply.

The agricultural possibilities of Alaska are not well known. The southern section raises some vegetables and even the Yukon valley has shown considerable capabilities for summer cultivation of quickly maturing plants.

The gold excitement will have a great tendency to call attention to Alaska's many other resources and to bear still further testimony to the wisdom of the once derided but now universally approved purchase of the country from Russia.

Epilogue

As did so may of those who were part of the great Klondike gold rush of 1996-98, author John Leonard just seemed to fade away without a trace.

He may have tossed away his pen for a pick and made his own fortune mining the creeks. Or he may have spent every penny he had in the dance halls of Dawson City. Or, then again, he may have moved along to Alaska, where many of the successive strikes occurred.

We do know, however, that thousands of hopefuls made their way to the Klondike during late 1897 and early 1898, many armed only with the advice provided by guide books such as this one. At its height, the gold rush attracted between 30,000 and 40,000 people to the Klondike. Dawson City was the second largest city in the west, next only to San Francisco.

Although most came north to mine the creeks, many came north to mine the miners. Some struck it rich beyond their wildest dreams, but most did not fare well and moved on to the next big strike or returned home empty-handed.

Those who did choose to stay in the Yukon after those two intense years kept the district alive for the next several decades. The population increased and decreased according to the price of gold.

Today, many people still make their living from placer mining in the Yukon. Gravel that would not have elicited the slightest interest in 1898 is now moved in large quantities to produce profits that usually makes it worthwhile. Some of the ground has been worked four — or more — times and is still offering up gold. "Gold fever" still strikes at the hearts of many and propels them onward in their own quest for riches.